ARTFUL PROFILES
OF
TROUT, CHAR, AND SALMON

and the Classic Flies That Catch Them

ARTFUL PROFILES
OF
TROUT, CHAR, AND SALMON

and the Classic Flies That Catch Them

Tips, Tactics, and Advice
on Taking Our
Favorite Gamefish

DAVE AND EMILY WHITLOCK
Illustrated by Dave Whitlock

Skyhorse Publishing

Skyhorse Publishing books may be purchased in bulk at special discounts for sales promotion, corporate gifts, fund-raising, or educational purposes. Special editions can also be created to specifications. For details, contact the Special Sales Department, Skyhorse Publishing, 307 West 36th Street, 11th Floor, New York, NY 10018 or info@skyhorsepublishing.com.

Skyhorse® and Skyhorse Publishing® are registered trademarks of Skyhorse Publishing, Inc.®, a Delaware corporation.

Visit our website at www.skyhorsepublishing.com.

10 9 8 7 6 5 4 3 2 1

Library of Congress Cataloging-in-Publication Data is available on file.

Cover design by Tom Lau

Print ISBN: 978-1-5107-3477-7
Ebook ISBN: 978-1-5107-3478-4

Printed in China

TABLE of CONTENTS

ACKNOWLEDGMENTS

When my approximately seventy-four years of loving, learning, and sharing this sport is combined with Emily's twenty-five years, I guess you could say we have about 100 years of this sport between us. All those years of living and breathing fly fishing have put us into countless personal and professional relationships with people who also love this sport. We'd like to thank all of them, as well as trout flyfishers, past and present, because they have had a role in the creation of this book. Thank you all for your influence, wisdom, and support.

First and foremost, I have to thank Emily Whitlock—for twenty-six years of such awesome care of my happiness and health. She has been a partner with me in all my work, and I couldn't do any of this without her. She has added to, edited, and improved everything I've written since we've been together—never complaining that all my manuscripts are given to her written out by hand. She is most responsible for my now full-time artist career and had a big hand in writing and editing this book.

Nick Lyons, renowned writer, editor of many of my books, and good friend, was the first to recommend to *Trout* magazine that they allow me to have a regular feature—and to write and illustrate just what I feel about the world of trout. The first body of these writings became the contents of my book *Trout and Their Foods*. Thank you, Nick, for your support and encouragement over our many years and for the innumerable good memories!

For many years, *Trout* magazine has provided us, and all trout flyfishers, a vocal and visual platform to gain more understanding about coldwater fishes, their habitats, their value to us all, and the many ways that we can preserve them. We appreciate that we've been allowed to contribute to this incredible forum for over twenty-five years. Keep up the good work!

Thank you, Kirk Deeter, editor of *Trout* magazine, for your outstanding encouragement for our writing and my art, and for being such a thoughtful editor of the articles that we submit. You are such a gentleman to work with and have supported this book every step of the way, and we are forever grateful.

Dr. Robert J. Behnke's devotion and contributions to our coldwater species has had a great influence on my biological understanding of trout and salmon. His incredible book *Trout and Salmon of North America* has been invaluable to me, and I recommend that every trout flyfisher who wants to truly understand these fish should have a copy of this book in their library. Dr. Behnke's book is illustrated by my trout art guru, Joseph R. Tomelleri. Joseph's outstanding technical pen, pencil, and paint portraits have helped with my efforts to achieve authentic anatomy and colors in the trout and salmon chapters of this book. Thank you, Joseph.

A big thank you to Mike Valla for his books *The Classic Wet Fly Box* and *The Founding Flies*. These books are so well written and were both such helpful references.

Davy Wotton, my dear Wales/Arkansas friend and renowned flyfisher, has generously helped with advice and historical information anytime

I asked. His perspective, especially on wet fly fishing, fly tying, fly tiers, and the history of fly fishing has helped make this book more authentic and colorful.

We want to thank and acknowledge the many Trout Unlimited chapters and members for the countless accomplishments in preserving, protecting, and improving North America's wild trout, char, and salmon population—past, present, and future.

Thank you to our very skilled book editor, Jay Cassell, for his most helpful advice, recommendations, and great editing. Let's do another one together, Jay!

—Dave Whitlock

FOREWORD

Whether you realize it or not, if you fish with flies, you have more than likely already been influenced by Dave Whitlock.

Just look inside your fly vest, or pack, or whatever you use to sling your gear to the water. I did that, just the other day.

In my right pocket, I found my "hopper box," and thumbing through that platter, I chanced upon a row of "Dave's Hoppers," and right below that was a row of "Whit's Hoppers." (I've found that the ones that have been chewed on a couple times actually work best, so they sit in the "go-to" spot in that box.) In the left pocket, I found a nymph case, as well as a small gaggle of streamer patterns . . . too many of which were concocted by Dave to list them all by name here, but suffice it to say, they account for many of the standards I turn to, over and over again, wherever I fish.

In my shoulder pocket, I found a handful of those nifty "Telstrike" indicators with a telltale post . . . another innovation from Dave that raises the game *just that much* higher. The more I thumbed around, the more Whitlock I found . . . but then again, that's all just "stuff."

Of course, "stuff" doesn't matter if one doesn't know how to use it, and Dave has done as much or more to explain how to fish, and more important, *why* certain "stuff" works, than anyone else. His *Guide to Aquatic Trout Food* and *Trout and Their Food* both sit on a permanent corner of my writing desk (right next to Strunk & White's *Elements of Style*). While there have been many wonderful authors who have penned worthy, lasting lessons on the "how-to" aspect of fly fishing, I honestly don't think anyone else has ever come as close to understanding and explaining the "why" of this sport—in scrupulous detail—as Dave Whitlock has.

And he has done so with artistic flair. What he is able to capture and convey through detailed, colored pencil drawings is unique and remarkable. Not only is he one of the preeminent teachers of fly fishing, he is also one of the great artists of the sport.

Several months ago, I stood in line by a booth at a fly-fishing show in Denver, to have Dave sign a copy of *Trout and Their Food* (granted, it was an extra). When he signed my copy (replete with an impromptu drawing of a brown trout and personalized inscription), he made the connection . . . you see, I've been his editor at *Trout* magazine (for Trout Unlimited) for the past five years. Naturally, once everything came into focus (I admittedly snuck up on him), we shared handshakes and hugs and all that . . . but he was that jovial and accessible and genuine with everyone in that line, before and after I showed up.

That's just Dave.

I've spent many years working very hard, writing and editing for *Field & Stream* and *Angling Trade* and elsewhere, to get to a point where I felt at home as the editor of *Trout*. And it was one of my great comforts when I assumed that position (actually, it blew me away) to know that I'd be able to work with Dave Whitlock on a column that still anchors that magazine.

But I cannot adequately express how satisfying and rewarding it is to get to a point where you get to work with someone you've always considered a hero, only to find out that that person is even more genuine, and gracious, and kind, and authentic than you'd ever hoped they might be.

That's exactly how I feel about Dave Whitlock.

When I'm working on issues of the magazine, it's often about shuffling sentences and fixing grammar, and cutting words to fit the column inches of space we've allotted to put the whole package together.

And sure, when Dave's pieces come in, I do my best to dot the "i's" and cross some "t's" here and there, but mostly, I just sit back and read. And learn. And I'm flabbergasted, every time, by just how much he's seen, and experienced, and understands. I'm even more amazed by how much of an "open book" he is.

I mean absolutely no disrespect to any of the "young guns" out there pushing the boundaries with new techniques and theories. Heck, I've aspired to be one of them for over twenty years now myself (which unfortunately takes me out of the "young gun" category). But no matter how edgy, or tough, or smart you may well be, you need to take a hard look at the lessons Dave Whitlock can share with you, because he's right,

and on the money. Always. And his lessons will stand the test of time, for as long as people endeavor to catch fish with flies.

Most important, Dave has a remarkable conservation conscience, and he's shared so much of his knowledge in the pages of *Trout* magazine for what amounts to pennies on the dollar. Just because he believes in the culture and the future of fly fishing, and he knows that without the resources, there is nothing for the angler.

So not only do I consider being asked to write this little foreword the highest honor of my writing career, I also speak on behalf of the hundreds of thousands of members and supporters of Trout Unlimited—who share that conscience and commitment to keeping our waters clean and our fishing great—in expressing our grateful appreciation to Dave for all he has done, and will do, for *Trout* magazine and beyond.

I hope you're able to tap the wisdom found in the following pages, and catch more fish, and further enjoy the sport. I hope you'll heed the voice, and I hope you'll endeavor to follow Dave's lead as a steward and mentor in fly fishing. You'll never, ever find a better star to lead your way.

—Kirk Deeter
Pine, Colorado, 2017

INTRODUCTION

For a lifetime, I've been held spellbound by wildlife, especially those that live in the water. More specifically, I'm drawn to fish, both cold and warm water. The cold-water species—trout, char, grayling, steelhead, Atlantic and Pacific salmon, and whitefish—are particularly fascinating to me. Each species in these groups is so unique and interesting, not only in fly-fishing terms, but in their anatomy, color patterns, life cycles, personalities, where and how they live, and what they feed upon. Every single one has a story to tell us about its watery life. If we know this story for each fish, our satisfaction and respect for the experience increases every time we briefly capture and release one.

With this book, it's my goal to share what I've learned about each fish and the flies that capture their interest. I hope to accomplish this by combining biological facts, my interaction with other flyfishers and writers, and my personal experiences of many days and years observing beneath the water, luring them to my flies and recreating their forms, colors, movements, and environment with my art. I'll choose the words for the texts, but perhaps even more informing will be my work to portray them with my inks, paints, and pencils. I've drawn wildlife and fish since I was a child, but a truly life-changing event occurred in my late teens when I bought a swim mask and fins. These simple tools allowed me to clearly see and discover the incredible wonder of the underwater world of streams. I clearly recall thinking that it was like discovering another world! It was so awesome to me that I have devoted most of my life to writing about and creating art to try to adequately share that wonder with others.

I'm often asked what I like to do most with my work time. That answer might surprise many of you who know my life as a professional flyfisher—I love creating the art most of all, especially these days. The paintings in this book represent many of the most vivid forms in my life experiences with these wonderful cold-water species. I hope they reveal not only the fish's form, colors, activities, and environment, but also the passion and respect I have for each of them.

When I was eight years old, I discovered fly fishing on a page of my granddad's L.L. Bean catalog! I remember it had a wooden fishing pole with red guide wraps, and next to it was an open sheepskin-and-wool book with several dozen hooks that had colorful feathers attached to them. I asked my granddad what these were, and he replied that those were "flies for fly fishing—a rich man's sport—not for us." Ever since that day I've been in love with flies, their histories, their creators, and with creating them myself. I hope, with my fly renditions and words, to give these wonderful, functional sculptures the historic and classic understanding they deserve. There are rich stories and endless forms, materials, and colors among them, and I can't tell you how much I've enjoyed this creative process.

One of the rewards I received while developing these families of historical and classical trout flies was the realization that they all remain timelessly effective to tempt trout and have never really become obsolete. The real beauty of flies is that they are our means, for a few brief moments, to make direct contact, capture, and behold the living treasures that live in the cold waters of our world.

For the last twenty-five years, Emily has been my loving companion in life, fly fishing, teaching, and all the aspects of my (our) work. She has been with me through many of the experiences I talk of in this book and right next to me helping to write and edit my articles, books, and videos.

I couldn't do any of this, including my artwork, without her invaluable partnership.

I hope after reading this book you'll come to know and see these fish and flies as we do—and know us better, as well.

PART ONE

PROFILES OF TROUT, CHAR, AND SALMON

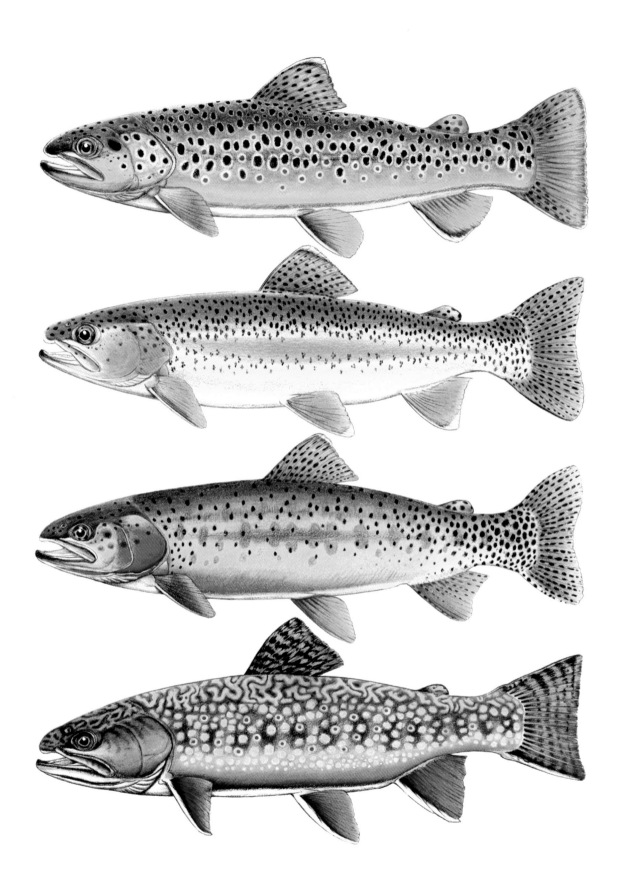

Four most common trout showing their most significant marking and color patterns.

CHAPTER 1

TROUT PROFILES

I've observed trout above and below the water surface all my fly-fishing life with unending fascination. Each species, its stream and still-water community, and even each individual fish, exhibits particular behavioral traits or "personalities." If we are aware of these, I believe our trout fishing and trout preservation become more meaningful, dimensional, successful, and satisfying. So, I'd like to share with you what my observations and experiences have taught me about how to *read* a trout.

Trout are among our most beautiful fish, and catching and cradling one in hand or net, just beneath the water's surface, never fails to thrill. As an artist, photographer, biologist, and flyfisher, my eyes have been trained to read each fish's physical history—its species, age, and sex, whether it is a wild or hatchery fish, in which phase of its life cycle it is in, its general health, and more.

Species identification is usually the first information we seek once a trout is hooked. If it appears to be silvery in the water with hints of pink, white, and olive, it's probably a rainbow. If it looks golden brown and yellow, it's most likely to be a brown trout. Coloration of deeper golden orange with lower fins of red usually means it's a species of cutthroat. A brook trout will reflect lower fins of orange or red and starkly edged in white and black.

After identifying the species, I usually try to determine the sex. For that I look at the head, especially the length of the lower jaw and general shape of the fish. Hen fish have short jaws that terminate with a compact, rounded nose and a slightly tapered lower jaw. The female's eyes appear to be larger than a male's of the same length. These characteristics give the hen fish a feminine look to me.

The male fish will have jaws that appear to be large and long and terminate with distinctive, hook-like upper and lower ends. The older and larger male jaws are so hooked, especially during spawning, that they are very fierce-looking. This testosterone-driven characteristic is known as the kype, and the teeth are usually large and relatively long. The male's coloring takes on a deeper chromatic intensity than that of females that

Opposite page: Rainbow: *back*—olive green; *side and side of head*—pink; *stomach*—whitish; *spots*—small, irregular black spots on head, back, sides, and dorsal and tail fins.

Brown: *back*—dark golden olive; *side and head*—yellow to bluish; *stomach*—yellow; *spots*—large black spots with distinct pale halos and crimson spots with pale yellow halos.

Cutthroat: *back*—dark golden olive; *side*—golden yellow and red; *stomach*—pale gold or cream; *spots*—small and black (larger and more spots on body near tail); fluorescent red slash on either side of head beneath lower jaw.

Brook: *back*—dark olive with gold worm-like markings; *side*—slate blue with distinctive parr marks; *stomach*—orange, black, and white; *spots*—pale yellow and crimson ringed with yellow and blue; *lower fins*—deep orange red with stark black and white leading edges.

are taken from the same water during the same season. With the less pronounced jaw of young male trout, you determine the sex by the deeper, more intense colors and spot patterns prominent in males. Young females will be paler in color and with less distinctive spots.

Both sexes lose their silvery sheens and become much more intensely and darkly colored as they begin their spawning runs. It takes about thirty to sixty days after spawning for these adults to become lightly colored again. Fall spawners take longer than spring spawners to recover the coloring and weight they lose during spawning because winter temperatures reduce their metabolism and less food is available.

Today, unfortunately, not all trout are created equal. Some are naturally born as wild trout, while many are products of our efforts to create sport fishing in areas where wild trout are scarce or nonexistent. So, when I catch a trout, I also like to identify if it is wild, a hybrid, or a hatchery product and, if hatchery raised, how long it has carried over. Many flyfishers likely experience a variety of types of trout wherever they fish across North America and elsewhere.

To me a wild trout has a look of perfection. The shape, fins, coloration, and performance are very distinguishing to these old, experienced senses. A wild trout will likely jump more often and fight a longer, stronger, and more enduring battle than a hatchery fish of the same size and weight. It will also feel very firm. These differences become less apparent if the hatchery fish has had six to twelve months' residence in the same

How to recognize hatchery and wild trout.

Top—Newly stocked hatchery trout (one to four weeks). Note the dull pewter color, soft, fat body, herniated rectum, fins and tail rays short and damaged.

Middle—Carry-over trout (three to twelve months in the river). Color starts to resemble resident trout, the body is more firm and lean, and the fins and tail are improving but still show scarring from hatchery life.

Bottom—Resident wild trout. Overall color is bright, body is very sleek and firm, all fins and tail are large and well shaped and often have white tips on the dorsal, pelvic, and anal fins.

waters as the wild trout. In the hand, a wild fish is beautiful! The brilliant colors, the markings, the eye expression, shape, and fins are perfection! If my first inspection has any doubt, I look to see if the fins are large and full; if there are few or no scars; if fins aren't split, torn, and ragged; and if there are subtle white tips on the fins. That would indicate to me a wild trout.

Recently stocked hatchery fish will have an overall dull, pewter-gray sheen and will feel slick and soft. Their fins, especially the pectorals and dorsal, will be scarred, ragged, and stunted from rubbing on other fish and the edges of the fish hatchery, from being bitten by other trout, and from sunburn and fungus fin rot. Some hatcheries also clip a fin to identify them as hatchery fish. Fortunately, this fin-clip maiming is being replaced by tattooing the gill cover, branding, or indicator nose implants. As these fish log time in the stream or lake, they gradually lose the gray dullness and take on a brighter metallic and more natural color. Usually, however, the fin disfigurement never completely goes away.

It's fairly simple to estimate the age of a trout. A trout less than one year old will seldom exceed six to eight inches and will have a row of oblong slate, pewter, or purple parr marks spaced along the lateral line. These marks usually fade and disappear with maturity. The exception is when trout are isolated in very small, very cold streams with little food base, where especially cutthroat, golden, brook, and brown, may maintain vivid parr marks and deep, rich color their entire lives. In old trout—between eight and twelve-plus years—coloration and markings become dull and muddied, and these old-timers tend to have more spots, thicker, rounded tipped fins, larger heads with longer jaws, and larger teeth.

Different habitats result in trout that look different. This is designed to give them the best

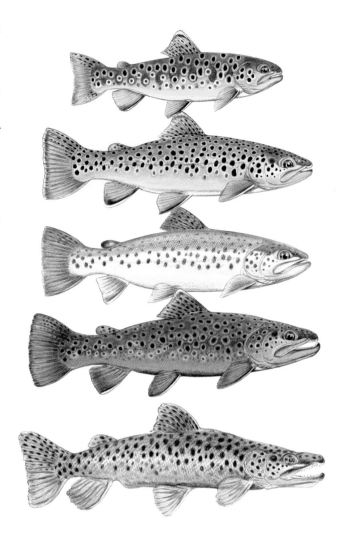

Brown trout colors (young to spawning).

Immature stream trout—small size with parr marks and simple but vivid spots

Mature stream trout—vivid colors and intricate spot patterns

Mature lake or sea-run trout—light- or chrome-silver color

Mature stream trout—full, rich spawning colors

Old trout—on the verge of dying

camouflage for that particular environment. Trout residing in relatively shallow, very clear and fertile freestone streams and rivers will have the most coloration, spots, and bright markings. If there is an abundance of crustaceans and aquatic insects to feed on, they will be even more colorful—outside and inside their skins. Trout raised in typical dark, crowded, concrete hatchery race-ways will be a drab pewter from back to belly. Trout living in silty streams will be pale colored, and those living in large clear lakes and oceans and those just returning from the sea will be almost colorless or silvery and possess few paler and smaller spots and markings.

In each type of water, trout simply adjust their coloration to mirror their environment so they are more difficult for air and water predators to detect. The scales, though tiny, are thousands of precisely positioned light-and-color reflecting and absorbing units that constantly function in all conditions to protect the trout. The back will always resemble the color of the water or stream bottom, making it harder for predators looking down from above to see them. Their sides will be most like the underwater coloration concealing them from aquatic predators at the trout's eye level. The underside is usually light colored, helping them to blend into the silvery appearance the water surface has when viewed by a predator from below.

When trout, char, and salmon begin their spawning activities, they become more color-ful, especially the males. Pinks turn to red; reds to deep crimson or purple; yellows change to deep-cadmium yellows and gold; and oranges and reds to burnt sienna. They often develop additional spots and can even change spot color from typical black to orange or red. By the com-pletion of the spawning, the head, side, and fin colors may fade into shaded, dull overtones, and their lower sides and stomachs can become pewter or black. After spawning and when food becomes abundant, these same fish will slowly return to their normal colors, sometimes taking two to three months. Because this spawning peri-od takes so much physical strength, it is some-times two or three years before they attempt the

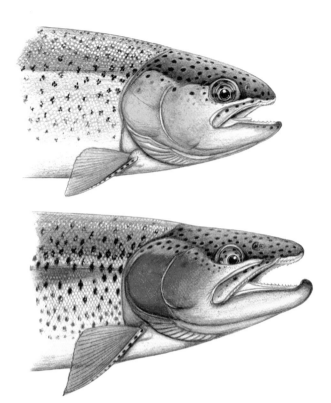

Trout sex ID.

Top—*female*. Head has relatively short jaws with large eyes near nose. Colors are more pearly and pale with smaller spots than males.

Bottom—*male*. Head has smaller eyes set well back from nose and long, pointed jaws with a distinctive hook on lower jaw. Overall color is vivid and chromatic, and the spots are larger and more distinct than those of females.

next spawn, especially older trout and char and migratory fish such as steelhead, Atlantic salmon, and sea-run trout.

A trout's health is easy to determine by shape, luster, skin condition, and flesh color. Healthy wild trout are firm feeling, have a definite luster to their scales and coloration, and their shoulder-thoracic area is somewhat larger than their head circumference. They are also active, long-winded fighters. When fish feel soft, or have lesions on their bodies, white spots on their

Eye-to-eye with a trout (top to bottom).

Trout in excellent condition—Eye is alert, moving, and pupil is focused.

Trout experiencing fatigue—Eye is fixed, pupil is dilated, and mouth is open and gasping.

Trout near death—Eye is lifeless, pupil is fully dilated and dull, and mouth is fixed open.

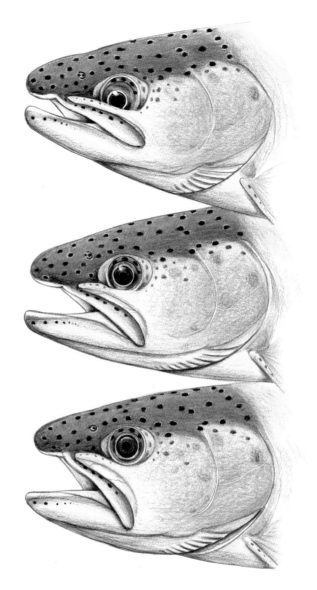

gill filaments or fins, eye cataracts, are skinny, or have flesh that is gray and mushy, they have health, food, or postspawning problems.

As an artist and flyfisher, I'd say that a trout's eye is the most important part to analyze. To determine a trout's existing or immediate physical condition—make eye contact with it. If the pupil seems to be focused and moves forward or down as you cradle the fish in your hands, it is fully conscious, alert, and ready to be released. If the pupil seems large and looks straight out, not down, it is likely in mild fatigue or shock and should be rested underwater, in hand, moving it gently back and forth into the current. When the pupil again becomes small and alert, it should be ready to release, but only if it swims off willingly. If the eye has a dull, "fish-eye" dilation and does not respond when you move the fish's head and it is breathing erratically or not at all, it is probably in deep shock and oxygen starvation and is dying or dead. Usually little can be done to save your fish at this point.

You can try patient, underwater respiration in flowing water and gentle body massaging to help restore oxygen intake. To avoid this critical condition, try to land the fish promptly with a catch-and-release net, keep the fish in the water, remove the barbless hook quickly and underwater if you can, and after it has a minute or so to rest and revive, let it swim out of your hands or net into a calm flow area. If you want a photo, hold the fish underwater until the photographer is focused and ready and then quickly hold the fish up for only a few seconds. As I've advised before, never keep a fish's head out of water any longer than you can keep yours underwater. Never toss any fish back into the water. It can cause additional survival problems with predators, water hazards, and disorientation—and it is disrespectful.

Each trout becomes more of an interesting treasure if we can recognize its individual characteristics. Each one is unique and has its own story to reveal. When I catch a trout, being able to identify the fish's age, stage, and condition can help me understand the population profile of the fishery and gives me a measurement of my fishing skills. If at the end of a day I've taken wild trout and/or well carried-over fish, it gives me great satisfaction and means I've probably used pretty good techniques.

With every painting of a trout I create, I take all these characteristics into consideration so that when you look at it, the painting will hopefully tell a story about its life.

CHAPTER 2

RAINBOW TROUT
(*Oncorhynchus mykiss*)

The rainbow is the most popular and widely available trout that we have in US waters. Although the native range is predominately the western slope of the Rocky Mountains, rainbows have been successfully introduced into practically every flowing and still water that can be classed as seasonal or annual trout-water habitat. Rainbows are certainly the most plastic of trout. Various strains or races have been "engineered" by federal, state, and private fish culturists to fit every conceivable sport fishing and market niche, even to the point of altering rainbows that normally spawn in the spring to fall spawners and the length of their life spans.

The first trout I ever caught was a Tennessee Smoky Mountain rainbow, using a cane pole and a bread-dough ball when I was seven years old. The first trout I caught on a fly rod and fly was a Missouri Roaring River State Park rainbow. At seventeen I caught my first wild trout—beautiful Montana rainbows. Since then, rainbow trout have given me countless fly-fishing pleasures over my lifetime.

Rainbows, true to their common name, are a rainbow of colors. Their backs and heads are usually the color of the water. Their cheeks and sides are pink to deep crimson rouge, and their lower body is usually white or a pale golden yel-

Rainbow trout are truly our classic image of a trout, especially when one flashes its pink stripe while rising to a surface fly in a dancing, foam-flecked riffle.

low. Seemingly countless black spots pepper their backs, sides, and fins. When rainbows spawn, their cheeks, sides, fins, and sometimes bellies become crimson red—especially the males.

Wild fish usually have long, graceful fins often tipped with white. Rainbows, from parr size to the lower twenty-inch range, are daylight loving and for the most part stay up on fin all day watching for food. I very seldom observe a rainbow resting on the bottom. If they have a choice of water to hold and feed in, it will be sunny riffles, runs, pockets, tail outs, pools, or still water, in that order. When I see swift, broken riffles and runs with lots of white bubbles, I automatically think "rainbow water." They will often swim with groups of other rainbows, cutthroats, or whitefish. Compared to other trout species, they appear to be happy-go-lucky wanderers, often moving to various areas of a section of stream or even wandering several miles each day. Rainbows also feed at night, but I've always seemed to catch fewer of them at night than during daylight hours.

Rainbows do not hesitate to feed on a wide variety of food at every level of their habitat. They love aquatic and terrestrial insects, crus-

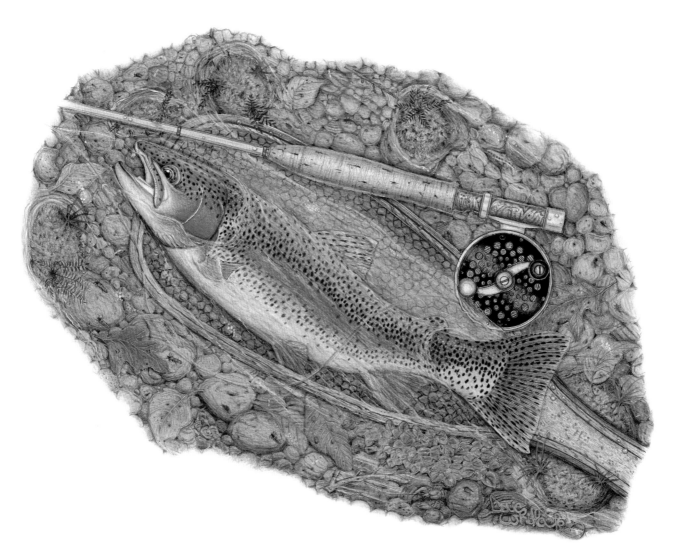

A mature male redband rainbow framed in a catch-and-release net is an awesome sight.

taceans, aquatic worms, and small minnows and sculpins. They seem to be the most willing species to respond and rise to a solitary floating food and are often the first to arrive to a hatch. They therefore are the ideal trout to cast a dry fly over during daytime hours and are nearly always willing to make a spontaneous rise to an Elk Hair Caddis, stimulator, hopper, Royal Wulff, or ant impersonator. That rise is usually a classic, flashy, quick up-and-down take, especially in rapid, riffle, pocket, and run water. Once hooked, rainbows will streak away from the pull and often quickly explode into leaps or tail walks, and then change direction and repeat their escape tactics, absolutely delighting our visual senses. Rainbows are our most aerobatic trout.

Mature rainbows, usually those twenty inches and longer, become more solitary, often focusing more on larger foods, such as sculpins, minnows, crayfish, and leeches, and seek lower light levels while feeding and resting. If they feed on surface insects, these more mature 'bows do so closer to stream shorelines and eddies. They prefer to hold in deeper and slower water, especially under the surface of a deep run. Structures such as submerged boulders, ledges, deep pockets, and aquatic plant beds are big rainbow areas. Here they will hold, usually suspended several inches off the bottom next to and, less often, beneath such structures. They will utilize submerged tree roots, stumps, and trunks for hides and feeding stations, but far less often than the other structures I've

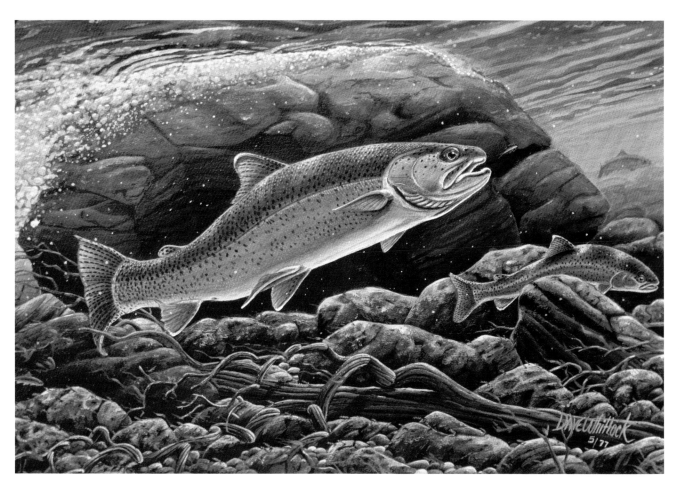

The rainbow's energetic open-water lifestyle makes this beautiful trout the perfect candidate for "most popular" cold-water sport fish.

mentioned. When hooked, rainbows will usually use open water in their escape attempts rather than swimming directly for hiding-beneath structures. This is good news for flyfishers who don't want to lose their fly or trout.

Rainbows seem to accept our intrusions into their world much easier than the more moody browns do. As a rule, they don't take very long to return to their feeding stations if disturbed by anglers and other nonnatural water activities. In fact, I have caught the same rainbow two or three times in one day often enough to believe that they soon resume their normal daily feeding activities if they are not traumatized by careless catch-and-release procedures. Having said that, I've also witnessed very selective rainbows that are almost impossible to hook even during a heavy hatch. The mature rainbows on the Harmon Ranch section of the Henry's Fork in Idaho are among the most selective and challenging to take on a

fly of any trout I've encountered anywhere in the world.

Recently stocked rainbows stay congregated and seek deeper, slower runs or pools. In high or swift water they easily fatigue and simply drift downstream. However, as they acclimate, they gradually strengthen, spread out, and begin to learn to find and use CSF zones (those areas that provide the good combinations of COMFORT, SAFETY, and FOOD). You can expect to find wild rainbows and those that survive stocking for at least a year well dispersed in CFS areas.

For flyfishers, rainbows are an ideal trout. They are usually active and eagerly feed well on a wide range of small food forms during daylight hours, especially in riffles, runs, pocket water, and the parameters of ponds and lakes. The rainbow's energetic, open-water lifestyle makes this beautiful trout the perfect candidate for "most popular" cold-water sport fish.

Rainbows are never hesitant to vault high above the water to catch a fast-flying caddis or eject a fly.

BROWN TROUT
(*Salmo trutta*)

I was seven years old when I saw my first brown trout. It was about fourteen inches long and on a stringer with rock bass, rainbow trout, and smallmouth bass that my dad had caught in a stream near Gatlinburg, Tennessee. It

The surface rise to a hatch that a brown makes is a smooth, graceful, carefully calculated sight that is many a dry flyfisher's ultimate pleasure. This is most likely why browns helped stimulate British Isles anglers to develop fly fishing.

stood out so distinctively from the others, with its big black and deep-red spots all along its bright orange-yellow sides, that I can still remember how it looked, even though I had no idea what kind of trout it was. Even today, every brown I catch seems unique, like a fascinating piece of original art. Of the fish species I photograph, illustrate, and paint, brown trout are my favorite subjects. For me they rival male ring-necked pheasants for brilliance and beauty. Their amazing color variations, the expression in their eyes, sheer size potential, gender differences, and lifestyles provide an artist or photographer an endless choice of subjects.

I've often heard that anglers evolve from first wanting to catch *a* fish, then *lots* of fish, next *big* fish, and eventually *intelligent* and *challenging* fish. Browns easily qualify for the last two goals of size and smarts—a wonderfully selective fish for the trout angler. They have a lifestyle that often allows some of them to survive up to eighteen years and thus grow big and old and wily, learning how to avoid many of the dangers associated with feeding.

The most outstanding example of this I've experienced are those amazing wild browns that inhabit the tailwaters of the White, Norfork, and Little Red Rivers in Arkansas. These stream-dwelling browns are increasing their populations, and many grow to world-record size, even while living in arguably the most intense bait-, conventional-, and fly-fishing pressure on this

Browns feed from bottom to top with a finesse that is mesmerizing to watch.

continent. A recent world-record brown was a seventeen-year-old fish caught in the Little Red River tailwater in Arkansas.

Brown trout eggs were legally imported to North America for introduction into our lakes and rivers in February of 1883. Fred Mather's Cold Spring Harbor hatchery on Long Island, New York, and Seth Green's hatchery at Caledonia, New York, received 80,000 eggs from Germany. Of these eggs, 60,000 were from large lake species and 20,000 from small stream species. Additional eggs arrived from Loch Leven, Scotland, in 1885, and more, still later, from England, Germany, and Scotland. Thus, many

browns are still termed German brown trout or Loch Leven browns, although there are few, if any, of these pure strains in our waters.

About this same time, in 1876, we received another gift from Germany—the common carp. Both browns and carp were introduced to enhance sport fishing and add to the food supply. Both have been highly successful despite both suffering verbal and physical persecution by anglers and fishing management authorities at different times over the years—each accused of outcompeting native species. For browns it was the eastern brook trout, Michigan grayling, and western cutthroat. They were branded as cannibals and "the

Browns usually seek protection and low light levels beneath aquatic vegetation, submerged stumps or logs, or large boulders and ledges.

worst thing that ever happened to native brook trout"! My years of angling experience and studies lead me to believe that the effect of human populations on native trout environments and "kill and keep" practices far overshadow predation and competition by browns and carp. Because both species are so adaptable and intelligent, they are often much more successful coping with human impacts on streams and lakes. By the way, all trout are predaceous cannibals on their own species.

It might surprise you to know that browns cannot tolerate higher temperatures than rainbows, with 84 to 86 degrees being their lethal limit. They can, however, handle a much wider pH range (4.5 to 9.8) with 8.0 seeming to be the pH in which they grow fastest and largest. This may be the reason that many of us have heard that browns can survive better than rainbows. Another misconception I often hear is that browns don't jump or fight as hard as rainbows. This fallacy would be quickly dispelled if folks were to learn that the brown's closest relatives are the landlocked and Atlantic salmon. My experiences in the Rockies, South America, Arkansas, and New Zealand have proven the opposite. A big, wild, stream-born brown will use every inch

Soon after young browns are stream born, they obtain their classic trademarks: golden-yellow sides vividly checkerboarded with inky-black and scarlet-red spots.

of the water, surrounding structures, as well as the air to separate itself from your fly and you.

Browns are generally more difficult to catch than are our native trout and char. Even those exiled to hatchery raceways display a standoff attitude. Tests show about a five or six rainbow to one brown catch ratio on average, stocked or wild. I'd add that's probably true on a good brown trout day, but that ratio can easily go to twenty or thirty to one on many of the waters I've fished, when browns are not active.

I've often read electroshocking reports that are lopsided toward the brown population in numbers and sizes, although many fewer browns were caught or sighted when fishing those waters. Here's why I think that happens.

Browns have two distinct behavioral personalities—one during daylight periods and another during low-light and dark periods. They tend to be daylight-shy trout that spend most of their nonactive periods avoiding direct sunlight on the bottom or beneath watery structures like ledges, boulders, stumps, logs, or moss beds. They pick only daylight hours that are highly productive to actively feed, such as during major aquatic insect emergences, like stonefly hatches (salmon flies, golden stones, skwalas, etc.), mayfly hatches (green drakes, tricos, PMDs, etc.), or when hoppers are active. They will also daytime feed when night water temperatures are too cold, such as in the Rocky Mountains. When they do rise to the surface during higher light levels, it's usually with very slow, careful, and deliberate rise forms—the kind of stuff that dry-fly lovers live for. You might say a brown's rise is a carefully orchestrated one, while a rainbow's seems much more impulsive.

After sundown, browns transform like Jekyll and Hyde. I've read of no other fish that has more acute night vision. They also have superior hearing and odor detection sensors, and they hunt at night—the owls of the rivers. They prowl miles of their territories, from top to bottom, boldly and aggressively seeking out prey, such as other fish, crayfish, large insects, mice, and so on.

When I was a young flyfisher, my holy grail was to catch on a fly a ten-pound, male, hooked-jawed brown with dime-sized spots. For twelve years I fished Montana, Wyoming, Idaho, Colorado, Missouri, and Arkansas blue-ribbon, brown trout streams without achieving that goal. Then I decided to try night fishing for browns. That first night, I caught my dream trout the first hour I spent wading the Missouri River after

Browns seem especially attracted, even on sunny days, to multiple wet flies fished actively toward the surface.

dark! All of the ten- to twenty-two-pound browns I've caught since have either been after sundown or on days when heavy overcast made it seem like evening.

Over the last ten years, I've become very excited about traditional European wet-fly fishing for browns, thanks to Davy Wotton's influence and teaching. It's a method, especially when using three size 10 to 14 flies, that seems to produce more browns in daylight hours than any other I've used. Davy and Roman Moser, both European flyfishers and intimately connected with brown trout, tell me it's because the active movements of the three flies are key triggers to the brown trout feeding stimulus. I've found the same in my own experience when using a big, actively fished streamer or sculpin. Lots of noisy, erratic action often causes browns to wake up and chase these fast-swimming flies. An additional action that works like magic on big browns is to suddenly change directions with a right or left line mend when the fish is following your streamer.

Brown trout are probably the fish that is most responsible for the development of fly fishing. Their beauty, selectivity, hard and cunning fighting ability, and wide and wild distribution make them the first choice for most trout fishers striving for those high goals of their largest fish and their most selective fish. Oh, by the way, when big, beautiful browns complete their lives here they reincarnate to the heavenly streams of New Zealand's South Island!

A common misconception is that browns don't jump—but, after all, the brown's closest relatives are the high-vaulting landlocked and Atlantic salmon. A big, stream-born brown will use every inch of the water and surrounding structures and lots of air to separate itself from you and your fly.

CHAPTER 4

BROOK TROUT
(*Salvelinus fontinalis*)

The distinctively marked and spectacularly colored *Salvelinus fontinalis*, or brook trout, is not actually a true trout but a char. Brook trout most likely got their name from the tiny, ice-cold brooks they inhabit throughout most of their native range, from eastern Canada down through the eastern United States—from Maine to Georgia. I've caught them in creeks so tiny you'd hardly believe a trout could exist there, as well as in beaver ponds, larger streams and ponds, big rivers, southern tailwaters, and huge northern glacial lakes. Brooks have also been successfully stocked in western streams but are generally considered to be competitive with native species.

Brooks, being char, do not have black spots but instead have lots of iridescent yellow or gold spots and numerous jewel-like crimson spots with pale-blue or lavender halos that seem to stand out above their skin. Complex vermiculations of worm-shaped metallic-gold and dark-olive camouflage markings cover their backs. From the side lateral-line down to the underbelly, the colors gradually spill over from blue or purple

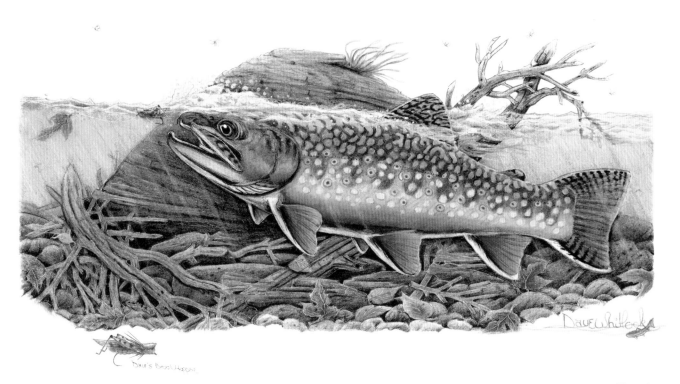

Brook trout have few rivals for intricate beauty and are wonderfully impulsive surface risers, especially to flies that have bright orange in the pattern.

to yellow, to orange, to black, and then to white. If you look closely, you can see the shadows of purple or blue parr marks beneath this complicated color pattern, especially in brooks under three years old. Iridescent white on the leading edges of the pectoral, pelvic, and anal fins contrast sharply with the sooty black and orange or red splashed across the majority of the fin rays. Their scales are so small they seem to be almost invisible, but if the sunlight hits them just right, they sparkle like tiny stars. To complete this carnival of unique coloration, the dorsal and caudal fins are each marked with black stripes over a background of golden olive to orange. In the fall, when brook trout are spawning, these colors become even more intense. The puzzle of this profusion of colors and markings is always

a great challenge for fish artists, wood sculptors, and taxidermists to duplicate.

Wild brook trout have a char's personality, which means that they tend to be aggressive, predaceous feeders. Brooks actively feed from the top to the bottom of the water column, and this vigorous feeding is often triggered by foods or flies that create some action, are of good size, and have bright colors. In their natural range, typical brook trout waters, though transparent, are stained from tannin, peat, and iron deposits to a golden, bourbon color. So it makes sense that big, bright, and active foods are probably the easiest for wild brooks to detect and capture. Because of their eager feeding habits, some label brook trout as gullible. I see it as an enjoyable product of their natural, aggressive char character.

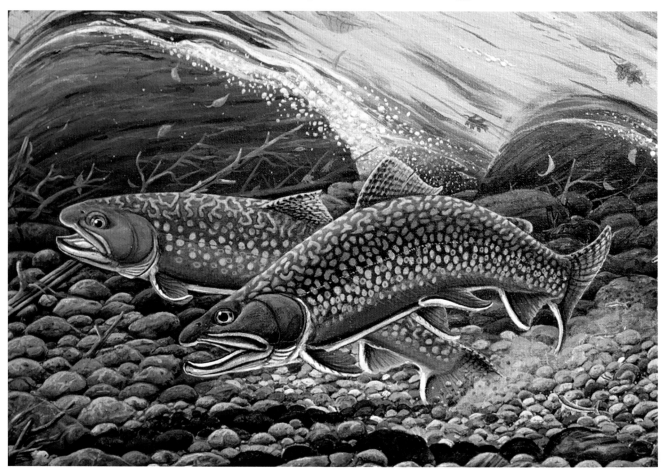

Brook trout become even more intensely marked and colored in the fall when they spawn. They are very adaptable to a variety of spawning areas, from still waters to tumbling brooks to boggy beaver ponds.

In my opinion, if there's one color to add to flies to almost ensure success in fishing for brook trout it would be fluorescent orange. They simply can't resist a dry fly, wet fly, or streamer with a flash of bright orange. A red-and-white combo would be a second good fly or lure color choice.

Over a four-year period in the 1980s, I had an opportunity to study Roland Reid's Osprey Lake brook trout fishery in Labrador, Canada. The fish in Osprey Lake were of the same giant race of brooks you hear so much about on the Minipi River fishery. To help Roland best manage this unique trophy fishery, I spent part of three summers tagging one hundred brooks each year in order to trace and record their numbers, growth rate, movements, and how often each fish was caught and released.

Most fish were caught in July and August and on large, colorful dry flies like the Royal Wulff. But often I'd get rises to my one-inch section of fluorescent fly line that I used as a strike indicator on my leader butt. It eventually became a real problem, and I had to remove the indicator. In time I caught on to this attraction and made a fluorescent-orange, fly-line bodied caddis, sizes 6 and 8, and my "Osprey Caddis" became the perfect tool to catch the one hundred brooks I had to tag . . . which averaged four and a half pounds and occasionally reached seven and eight pounds!

In the 1980s I was also involved with the L.L. Bean fly-fishing schools, and one of the most popular brook trout flies for Maine and most other eastern brook trout waters was a Dave's

This brook spawning pair scene was one of my very first attempts to capture these beautiful fish in the environment beneath the surface of a stream.

Hopper tied with a fluorescent-orange body and orange kicker legs.

Some of the favorite foods of brook trout are earthworms, sculpins, aquatic insects, leeches, crayfish, minnows, and mice, as well as other brook trout. While doing an advanced Atlantic salmon and brook trout school at Labrador's Eagle Lake, one of the lodge's native guides caught several two-and-a-half- to three-pound brooks for our lunch. Some unusual-looking lumps distorted the stomach of one of the trout. These lumps turned out to be three moles! Where, why, and how that trout caught moles is still an amazing mystery to me.

That reminds me of another brook experience on that same trip. I was trying to catch some of the huge pike we often saw stalking the brooks as we brought them in to tag. I was using an eight-inch, yellow and fluorescent-orange bucktail streamer that I'd tied for bluefish! Unfortunately, I hung up and had to break it off. Not long afterward I saw my big, eight-inch streamer swim by me in the mouth of a four- or five-pound brookie. He was carrying it crosswise, like a dog carrying a bone!

Although occasional trophy-sized, four- to eight-pound brook trout are taken in larger eastern US waters, especially during summer evening Hex hatches or spring smelt runs, most native brooks are more likely to be four to eight inches long and live in beaver ponds, spring-fed bogs,

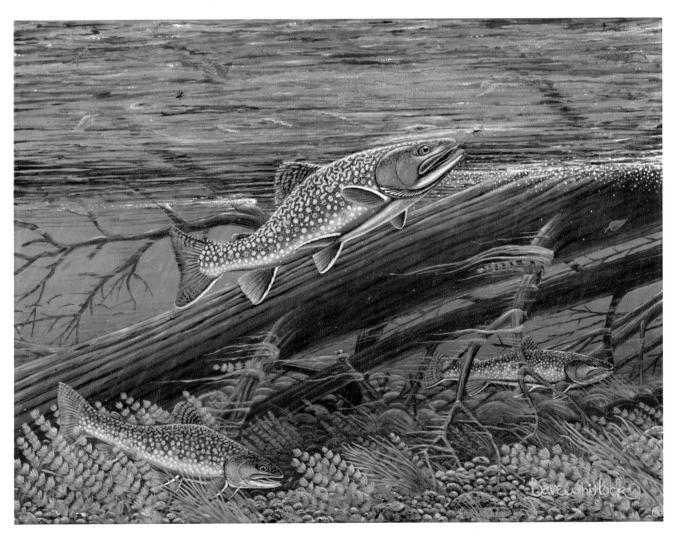

Brook trout are attracted to woody structures such as root wads, fallen trees, and logs.

and the tiniest of ice-cold streams. Here, one's day is a success if a ten- or twelve-inch brook is taken on a fly.

These awesome little jewels, tucked away in the most remote mountain tributaries and living secretly just on the edge of existence, are special hidden treasures. Folks that use 7-foot, 3-weight rods and make short roll casts under thick rhododendron canopies to secretive brooks have a real fly-fishing love affair with these wonderful wild char trout.

A good friend in Georgia told me about a small population of tiny brook trout that live precariously, high up in the mountains, in the upper last several hundred yards of a tiny, low-fertility stream that tumbles through his property. He said that once brookies were very plentiful throughout the full ten or twelve miles of the stream, but fishing pressure, as well as stocked brown and rainbow trout, consumed or displaced nearly every brook trout except for this handful of tiny,

beautiful natives at the top of the stream, where few of the nonnatives ventured.

This unfortunately has been a common occurrence in much of the brook trout's natural range, along with the negative impact of acid rain and global climate change.

Brooks prefer water temperatures between 45 and 60 degrees Fahrenheit and seem equally comfortable in still, flowing, and fast pocket waters and, amazingly, are able to spawn well in all these locations. They like to hang close to shady water structures, much like browns do when lying low in bright light, and feed mainly during the lower light hours. They can be spooked but can soon forget why and return to their feeding territory. They seldom jump after being hooked, though they rise to the surface freely for floating and flying foods. In fact, I've had small ones jump out of the water and catch my dry fly before it even hit the water. They are strong and dogged fighters. By all means use a catch-and-release net

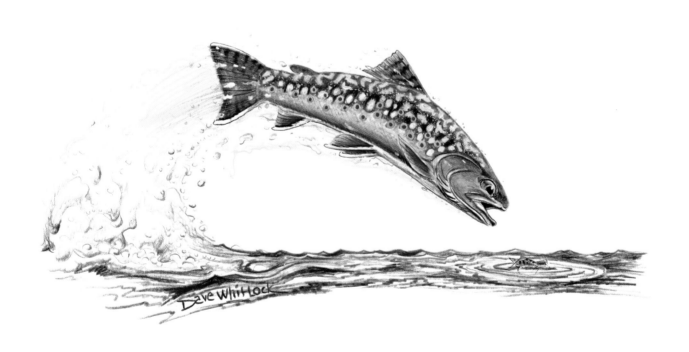

Small brook trout living in remote small creeks and beaver ponds will, without hesitation, dash up and out to snatch a dry fly or hopper.

on them, as they have a mouth loaded with needle-sharp teeth and an extra-slick, smooth body that's almost impossible to hold onto when they are alive and wet.

My favorite brook trout flies are black, yellow, and orange Marabou Muddler; Osprey caddis; orange-bodied Dave's Hopper; paradun Hex; olive, black, or brown Marabou Leech or Woolly Bugger; mouse rat; orange NearNuff Crayfish; and damsel and dragon fly nymphs.

I always jump at the chance to try for these beautiful, aggressive trout because they are so exciting to experience with my fly rod, my camera, my paintbrush, and my eyes.

CHAPTER 5

CUTTHROAT TROUT
(*Oncorhynchus clarkii*)

One of my favorite trout to catch, photograph, and paint is the cutthroat, especially the gorgeous Yellowstone, greenback, and westslope varieties. But then I can't leave out those lovely "cuts" in the rivers of Colorado. They all have a unique brilliancy that makes each catch an awesome event!

Most of the four groups that represent the fourteen individual subspecies of cutthroat trout have numerous small black spots, golden-olive to green backs, gold-plated flanks sometimes with tints of rose, crimson gill plates, and lower fins colored from rich cadmium yellow to deep crimson. All display either orange, pink, or red slash marks on their lower jaws. The cutthroat's colors are especially vibrant in mature males during their spring spawn. At that time it's easy to mistake them for golden trout or Kern River rainbows. More chroma is also usually present if there is an abundance of crustaceans in their diets, especially shrimp, Daphnia, and crayfish, as well as certain aquatic insects. Trout will almost always have more vivid colors and pronounced markings if they live in very clear, shallow-water streams that have colorful stone bottoms.

I was surprised to learn from Robert Behnke's remarkable book *Trout and Salmon of North America* that, at one time, cutthroat had the largest natural distribution of any North American trout, char, or salmon except the lake trout. I was not surprised to learn that cutthroats evolved from rainbow trout because, to me, they have so many similar external and internal physical traits. But unlike wild rainbows, cutthroats don't jump, cartwheel, or tail walk. They just seem to be more mellow. Maybe that's the reason they don't explode above the surface like the speedier 'bows.

Having said that, what cutthroats lack in aerial talents they more than make up for with how

My four favorite cutthroats to catch, photograph, and paint. Top to bottom: Colorado River, westslope, greenback, and Yellowstone.

The surface rise of a cutthroat is a thing of beauty.

beautifully and deliberately they take subsurface and surface flies and how relentlessly they battle. In my opinion, only a very selective brown is in the cutthroat's class for sensuous surface rises to a hatch, ant, or hopper. The surface rise and take of a cutthroat is a thing of slow-motion perfection and beauty. In fact, it's often difficult for the inexperienced flyfisher to wait long enough before striking a precisely timed cutthroat's surface rise. I remember enjoying Saturday mornings watching classic cutthroat rises on ESPN's *Fly Fishing American*. They produced several episodes that perfectly captured the cutthroat's measured, easy rises to dry flies and hoppers.

For some flyfishers, cutthroats and brook trout have reputations of being dumb or gullible. But that's not correct for either fish, especially once they begin to experience fishing pressure and catch-and-release regulations. I remember years ago, before catch and release was implemented on the Yellowstone River in the park, I could hook many, many cuts in one day on a size 4 black Woolly Worm. When these fish had to be returned to the river after catch and release, they

wised up quickly, and soon I needed to precisely match emerging insects to do well. An upside is that I had to improve my fly-fishing skills—and that's a good thing!

After the fine-spotted Snake River cutthroats were stocked in Arkansas's White River and Norfork tailwaters, I was amazed at how selective, secretive, and spooky they soon became compared to hatchery rainbows and even most of the browns there, and how fast they grew. I hooked one several years ago on a very large sculpin streamer that I first thought was a big brown, but it was an eight-pound male cutthroat. What a thrill. That fishery today is undergoing another cutthroat subspecies enhancement. The Arkansas White River Trout Unlimited (TU) Chapter 698, with help from other groups, has introduced the Bonneville cutthroat into the Norfork and Bull Shoals tailwaters using the Whitlock-Vibert trout hatching boxes. In a very short five years (2012–2017), wild Bonnevilles between ten and twenty-one inches are being caught on a regular basis. These uniquely spotted cutthroats are now depositing their own eggs in the river!

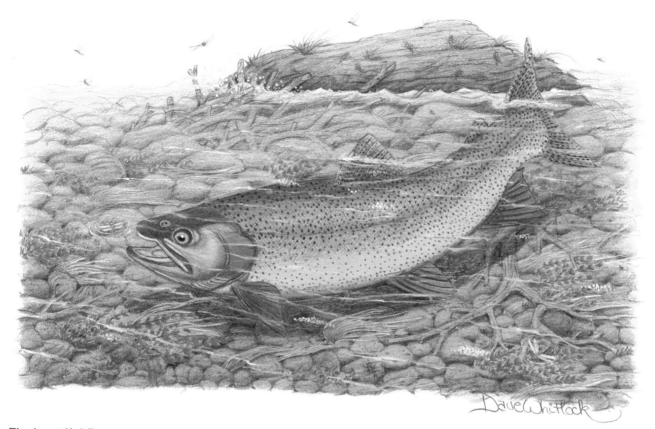

The beautiful fine-spotted cutthroat is native to the Snake River system in Idaho and Wyoming and has been successfully introduced in other waters.

In the Yellowstone River between the Yellowstone Lake outlet and Yellowstone Falls, as well as on Slough Creek and on the Lamar River, you can find some of the most marvelous, classic surface fly fishing anyone could ever expect to have for wild fourteen- to twenty-inch native trout! These are blue-ribbon opportunities that I try to never miss when I'm near the park in August, September, or October.

Cutthroats seem to use most of a stream's food-rich habitat, with riffles, runs, and tail outs being their favorites. They love structure and boulders, ledges, moss beds, logs, root wads, and coarse rock shorelines, all of which attract cuts. The two monster river cuts I've caught in my life were both living beneath the flooded trunk and limbs of big fallen trees.

It's my belief that cutthroats, like the always-eager rainbows, love to be up on fin, feeding during daylight hours, which, of course, is usually the most pleasant time to be wading in a lovely stream. But if hatches intensify toward and after sundown, they'll feed away all evening.

The best cutthroat flies are those that imitate the most abundant live foods in the waters. Aquatic and terrestrial immatures and adult insects probably top the list, but cuts also readily feed on small fish such as sculpins, shiners, small trout parr, smelt, dace, and threadfin shad. Scuds, damsel and dragonfly nymphs, backswimmers, leeches, flying ants, and grasshoppers are the choicest foods to imitate in still-water beaver ponds, sloughs, and lakes.

Cutthroats stay up on fin and feed equally well from surface to middepth to bottom, preferring aquatic insects.

The common name "cutthroat" was probably first used in 1884 to describe the black-spotted trout that Charles Hancock, editor of *Forest and Stream*, caught in Rosebud Creek, a tributary of the Yellowstone River in Wyoming. He described the trout he caught there as having an intense slash of carmine across their lower jaws as large as his little finger, and so he called it the "cut-throat trout."

Cutthroats were the first trout encountered by major European explorers of the West. In 1541, Pedro de Castañeda de Nájera, a member of Coronado's expedition, in search of the mythical city of gold, discovered something more special than gold: the Rio Grande cutthroat. In 1805, the Lewis and Clark Expedition caught the westslope

cutthroat on the Missouri River below Great Falls, Montana.

If you decide to explore the West soon, I certainly hope that cutthroat will be the first native western trout you discover with fly rod, camera, or paintbrush. A special quest could even be catching, photographing, and releasing as many of the fourteen cutthroat subspecies as you can find.

If you'd like more technical information about the amazing cutthroat trout, as well as all other North American trout, char, and salmon, I'd recommend you read *Trout and Salmon of North America*, expertly written by Robert Behnke and beautifully illustrated by Joseph Tomelleri and published by Free Press (2002).

CHAPTER 6

GOLDEN TROUT
(*Oncorhynchus mykiss aguabonita* and *Oncorhynchus mykiss whitei*)

Golden trout, especially the Volcano Creek golden, are one of the world's most rare, colorful, and beautifully marked trout and have always enthralled me. They are a flyfisher's and artist's dream to catch and photograph. Thank goodness for those vivid and clear photos and paintings, because otherwise few folks would even recognize goldens. These wild-living trout are among the most remote in the United States, living very isolated in tiny, icy-cold streams and natural lakes, usually above the tree line in the thinnest atmosphere. They seem to flourish best above 10,000 feet, making it very difficult for most of us to get to them. But just knowing such magnificent trout exist is a wonderful feeling for trout fishers and nature lovers alike.

When wild trout live at high altitudes where the waters are crystal clear and exceptionally clean, they are exposed to a high level of the sun's

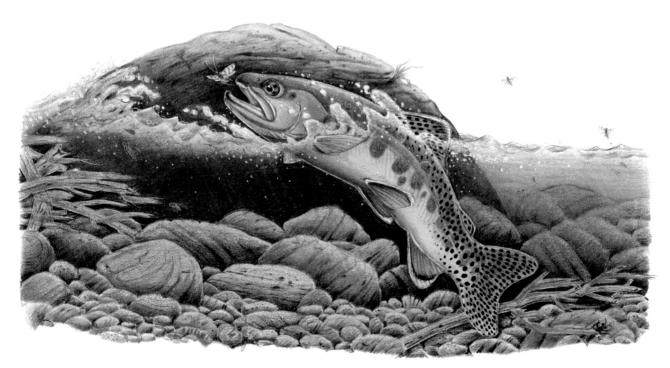

Goldens are fast, spontaneous risers looking for any natural food that becomes available—or flies that suggest food. Each six- to sixteen-inch wild golden trout is a beautiful treasure from nature.

radiation. These streams are usually lacking algae growth and silt, and so the stream bottom rocks are clean and often gemstone colorful. As a protective response to the intense sunrays and the colorful surroundings, these high-living trout are always brilliantly and deeply colored and marked. The Volcano Creek golden, particularly the mature males close to spawning season, will challenge your senses with their chromatic vividness.

The backs of these fish are a perfect mix of pure gold and light olive, blending into a glowing cadmium yellow on the sides. Slashed along their lateral line and belly is a fiery orange red that is unique to this subspecies. Over the back and sides is often a row of nine to twelve olive or violet-pewter parr marks starting just behind the deep-crimson gill plate all the way to the tail. Add to that pectoral, pelvic, and anal fins that are marked and colored in orange, white, and black that even surpasses the gorgeous brook trout. As a final finish, the upper body and ivory white-tipped dorsal and caudal fins are overlaid with

Golden trout only occur naturally in the alpine streams of the Sierra Mountains. They are vividly colored trout, and when spawning their colors defy even an artist's description. I painted this scene using two photos of goldens that a friend caught, one of the male and one of the female.

large, wonderfully distinctive ebony-black spots. Like wild brook trout, goldens have tiny scales that, in sunlight, look like twinkling galaxies of golden stars.

The golden trout is the Golden State's (California's) state fish and is now closely protected in most of its native High Sierra Mountain range. This helps prevent threats of hybridization with rainbows and deadly competition with exotic brown and brook trout. A close look at the Kern River golden clearly shows its recent ancestry with coastal rainbows, while the Volcano Creek golden is still more purely how trout enthusiasts picture a golden trout.

Shortly before 1939, when exportation of golden trout eggs and fry became prohibited by California, goldens were successfully established in remote high-altitude lakes and small streams in the Beartooth Mountains of Montana and the Wind River Range of Wyoming. Today, California has some three hundred golden trout waters. If you want to catch wild goldens in any of the remote locations where they thrive, you'll need to get your feet, legs, back, butt, and lungs in shape—big time.

Goldens were initially native to only small, high-altitude streams, but they have been successfully introduced to lakes in these same areas of the Sierras. They grow larger in lakes. In most streams a "nice" golden would be eight to twelve inches and just fit nicely into the palm of your hand, but the state and world records of nine pounds eight ounces and eleven pounds were both caught in food-rich lakes.

Goldens act and feed much as do wild rainbows and cutthroats. They are quick and nimble swimmers and use the entire water column to dine, favoring mayflies, caddis, midges, and stoneflies in streams. High-altitude waters are usually cold, swift, and relatively infertile, so goldens in these types of streams must be opportunistic and impulsive so as not to miss a chance at a meal. So, a good cast with a reasonable presentation of a buggy fly will often get instant rises. These little beauties hang out in riffles and runs, especially around larger rocks, cut banks, and beneath overhanging brush. In lakes they cruise shorelines to eat abundantly on midges, Daphnia, water fleas, scuds, and damselflies.

Ralph Cutter, in his *Sierra Trout Guide*, recommends using Royal Trudes, black ants, Elk Hair Caddis, Adams, and gold-ribbed flies for goldens. I'd add Dave's Damsel Nymph, Royal Wulff, Red Fox Squirrel Nymph, midge larvae, and scud patterns when tempting golden trout in still waters.

An ideal tackle setup for typical stream goldens would be a 7- to 8-foot, four-piece, 3-weight fly rod, a 3- or 4-weight double-taper floating fly line, and a 7½-foot 4X or 5X leader. This setup will also work if you plan to fish lakes, but I'd carry an extra spool with a 3-weight, clear intermediate line for still-water nymphing. A waterproof digital camera is indispensable to capture the incredible golden experience. I like to use a small, wooden-handled catch-and-release net laid in the stream to safely rest and frame a golden's portrait. Lay your rod across the edge of the net to enhance the shot.

I've often written that a wild trout is a true treasure. In the case of a wild Volcano Creek golden trout, they are more precious than California panned gold, in my opinion. And with goldens, remember it's not the size or the number, it's the total experience: the anticipation; the preparation of body and equipment; the rare air, clear sky, gorgeous mountains, alpine sounds, and smells that perfectly frame your breathtaking sight of a wonderfully wild, live golden trout across the palm of your wet, icy stream–chilled hand.

I'd recommend getting a copy of Ralph Cutter's exceptionally informative and beautifully illustrated *Sierra Trout Guide*, published by Frank Amato in 1991, as a must-read and complete reference guide to your future golden trout plans and success. And remember, every mile you hike farther from the road in golden country, the better your experience will be.

When I think of miniature golden trout enjoying a pristine alpine stream life, I always envision one jumping for joy with a big, happy expression!

CHAPTER 7

APACHE TROUT
(Oncorhynchus gilae apache)

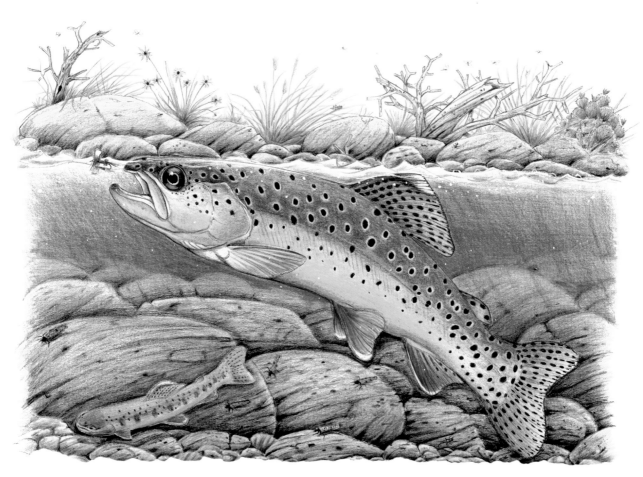

The vividly colored and marked Apache trout live in the White Mountains of Arizona in high-altitude, small tributaries of the White, Black, and Little Colorado Rivers. These six- to nine-inch little torpedoes rise freely to small dry, wet, and nymph flies.

The rare and beautiful Apache trout, also called Arizona trout, inhabits only 600 miles of tiny, fragile Arizona streams above 6,000 feet. This trout—called yellow trout by some locals—is a close relative of the Gila trout (sharing the *gilae* species) and is listed as threatened under the Endangered Species Act. Its existence is tenuous, mainly in high-gradient, low-fertility, headwater streams of the White, Black, and Little Colorado Rivers. Its struggle to survive is made even harder because its native waters are subject to droughts, fires, floods, high temperatures, and invasions of introduced rainbows, browns, and brook trout.

We should be thankful that the White Mountain Apache Tribe, the state of Arizona, Trout Unlimited, and fly-fishing groups such as the Arizona Flycasters Club are going all out to preserve the pure Apache strain and provide the fish with better habitat, less competition, and supplemental hatchery stockings of eggs, fry, and catchable fish.

In fact, it was an Apache trout fundraiser sponsored by the Arizona Flycasters Club that took me to Phoenix and then to the White Mountains and my first opportunity to catch an Apache trout on a fly. A group of us assembled at Christmas Tree Lake, one of the man-made lakes constructed and stocked with Apache trout by the White Mountain Apache Tribe on the White Mountain Apache Reservation. We used float tubes to access this lovely small lake, and fishing was excellent! The golden-backed residents that seemed to glow against the lake's dark bottom were especially attracted to, of all things, my bright-yellow Force Fins, and following in the fins' wake, they eagerly snapped up the damsel nymph imitations I presented to them. Some were seventeen to twenty inches long, and I was pleased at how well they fought and how they looked very much like cutthroat in my net. Upon closer inspection it was clear, though, that their shape, fins, and spotting were truly unique to my artist's eye, and they began to look more like maybe a hybrid of a Yellowstone cutthroat, a female Montana grayling, and a brown trout! That's because their backs, sides, and stomach were a varying dark to light golden yellow, the

distinctive prominent black spots had brown trout–like golden halos, and the dorsal fins were the longest rayed I'd ever seen on a trout. I've never seen any mention of that unusual Apache dorsal fin shape and size in any literature. Joe Tomelleri has accurately illustrated it, however, and there is a similarly shaped and colored dorsal on the Mexican golden trout in Robert Behnke's *Trout and Salmon of North American*. I've tried to recreate what I saw in this illustration of a feeding Apache trout.

My host, Ron Thomas, was quick to inform me that the wild, stream-bred natives were lean and quick, six- to nine-inch miniature replicas of the fat-cat hatchery releases. Later I was surprised to learn that these small-stream Apache adults only spawn between 70 and 200 eggs. This small number is another amazing example of nature's ability to adjust size and numbers to fit the environmental limits.

Wild Apache trout seldom, if ever, show the parr marks that other trout have as parr or young adults. They do have vividly white-tipped dorsal, pelvic, and anal fins. If you look closely at their eye, it appears to be masked in black because of spot-like pigmentation immediately in front of and behind the pupils.

Apache trout living in their small natural streams hold close to deeper pockets and bottoms but rise with little hesitation to any small, unlucky invertebrate from the top to the middle of the water column. Size 16, 14, and 12 nymphs and dry flies fished with a 7- or 8-foot, 4X or 5X leader on 7-foot, 3-weight rods are ideal for hooking this unique, beautiful fish in its natural environment. A catch-and-release net will help you capture and make a prompt release of any you bring in.

For the reservation lakes, where the Apache grows much larger and has unlimited space and

depth to forage, a 5-weight, 9-foot rod, combined with floating or clear intermediate fly line and size 12 to 6 leeches, damsel nymphs, and Woolly Buggers is most effective. However, when calm, these small lakes fish well on the surface with midges, ants, and caddis.

If you want to notch your rod handle with another unique trout, travel to the Arizona White Mountains and the White Mountain Apache Reservation, where Apache trout exist in their native waters. The area is lovely, and this little trout is the crown jewel of these waters. Be sure to take some digital photos of your trout, cradled in a catch-and-release net and lying in the stream flow. You'll have a cherished memento of one of our rarest and uniquely beautiful trout. For more information on Apache trout waters and fishing regulations, visit azgfd.gov.

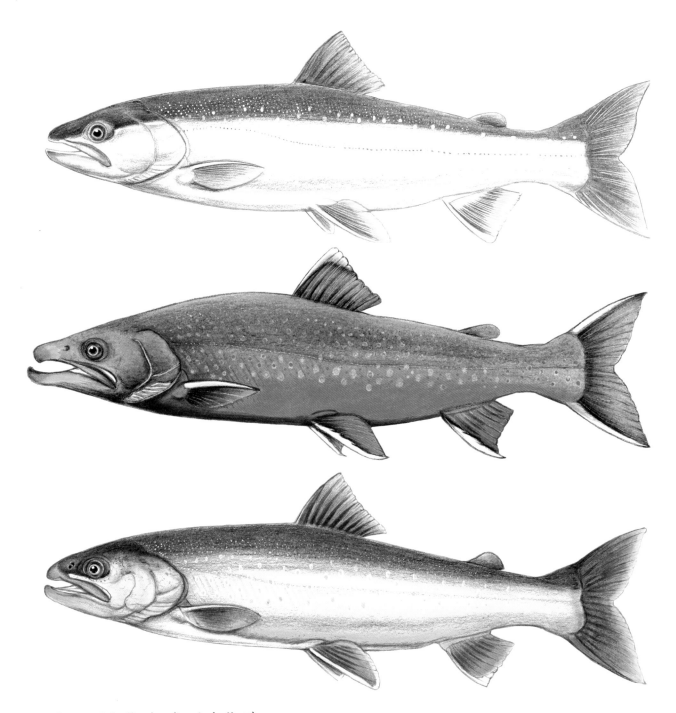

Color forms of Arctic char (top to bottom):

Arctic char living in the Arctic ocean or large Arctic lakes.

Spawning male.

Nonspawner living in freshwater streams.

CHAPTER 8

ARCTIC CHAR
(*Salvelinus alpinus*)

Arctic char are very well named, as they have evolved to thrive in some of the world's most frigid, ice-laden, and hostile places—the streams, lakes, and rivers of Europe and North America's Arctic. The size, complexity, and harsh climate of their native waters have resulted in many different and unique populations that are still a mystery in many ways to both science and anglers.

Char, in the arc of North America's Arctic region, exist as three separate and complex subspecies. The *oquassa* can be found in the most northern New England states and southeastern Canada. Three groups of char within this subspecies are the Sunapee, blueback, and Quebec red trout. Anglers fishing Labrador's most northern waters for Atlantic salmon, brook trout, and lake trout may also have an opportunity to take *oquassa*.

The subspecies *erythrinus* includes the giants of the Tree River and live in the northernmost Arctic. Taranetzi populate northwestern Alaska, south of the Kenai Peninsula, Kodiak Island, and the Alaska Peninsula and is the subspecies that is most often taken by anglers fishing Alaskan waters for Pacific salmon, steelhead, rainbow trout, and Dolly Varden.

All three subspecies have populations that live only in the freshwater of their home stream or lake as well as populations that are anadromous, in that they go to sea for brief periods of feeding. The anadromous forms are always larger because of their abundant food and space advantage. Many

Arctic streams and lakes are frozen over for all but two or three months of the year, providing very limited food production for the resident char.

When most anglers think of Arctic char, they recall the yard-long, eye-popping, and brilliantly crimson-colored Tree River char often held up by well-known, world-class anglers that appear in fishing magazines. But flyfishers who have actually caught Arctic char in their natural range know that most are much more likely one to four pounds and moderately colored.

Populations of Arctic char vary considerably in age, color, and shape. Most that I have caught or seen are strong but very sleek and slender in shape. The tails are noticeably more forked than those of other trout and char, except for lake trout. When not in spawning colors, they have olive to bluish-green backs, pink to pearl sides, and white bellies. The fins are usually colorful light yellows or rich oranges, and the pelvic and anal fins have bright white borders. Char have background spots that are larger and paler than those on Dolly Varden, usually colored from white to pale pink or lavender.

Spawning colors are the crowning glory of the char. At six to eight years, most Arctic char mature and spawn. The males develop a distinctive, orange-colored kype and a vivid orange to crimson body coloration that rivals the male sockeye salmon. Pelvic, pectoral, and anal fins and the lower tail all become vividly marked with white, black, and crimson. The spots seem

Because most Arctic char live in very cold water, they have limited food sources and a short growing season and are therefore opportunistic feeders by necessity. An array of eggs, brightly colored streamers, prawns, and sculpins should reliably catch them.

to almost pop off their sides with fantastic, fluorescent-red centers.

When I've fished in rivers with spawning char, I've noticed that less than half the males actually wore the spawning colors. Due to the frigid water conditions of their natural range, it takes most mature Arctic char three to four years to develop each successive reproductive cycle. This alone should tell us how susceptible these beautiful fish are to imbalances in their habitat.

By absolute necessity, Arctic char are opportunistic feeders on aquatic invertebrates, fish eggs and fry, crustaceans, and forage fish such as smelt. But even so, their growing season is very short and their growth very slow. One of the few exceptions are the char in Canada's Tree River system. The unique configuration of the estuary and river allows the fish to feed in the ocean and then for a more extended period in the river than is common for other char, thus providing a much longer growing season. Instead of a one- to four-pound average, these Tree River char average ten to twenty pounds and the largest on record is thirty-two pounds nine ounces, caught in 1982.

All trout, salmon, and many other char species are classed as cold-water fish, with their best

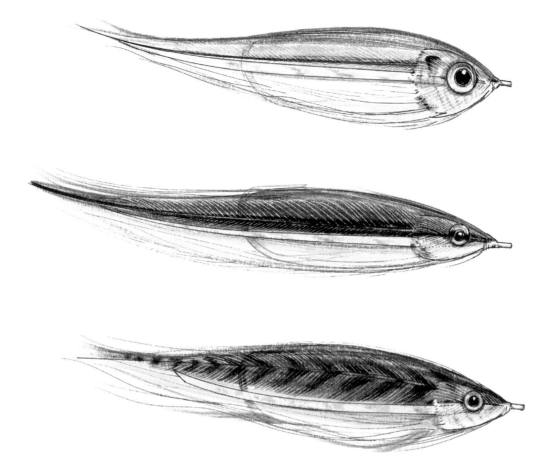

Most mature members of the char family prefer to feed on minnows such as shad, dace, and yellow perch.

comfort range being between 45 and 65 degrees Fahrenheit. Arctic char are most comfortable at a frigid 30 to 45 degrees—a temperature that would freeze most trout in their metabolic tracks!

Arctic char will readily take artificial flies and lures that imitate salmon eggs and small fish and are occasionally caught on nymphs and dry flies. Colorful, barbless, single-hook streamers or spoons and spinners, fished near the stream bottom and moved with the classic across, down, and around swing, are the most consistent producers.

Because char are so aggressive, considered good eating by many, take so long to mature, and do not reproduce yearly, it is easy to have a negative effect on wild populations. So, I urge you to practice catch and release of these beautiful, incredibly hard-fighting Arctic treasures 100 percent of the time.

Because of the remoteness and extreme northern latitude of the char's native range, there is still much to be learned by anglers and biologists alike about this most interesting fish. If you'd like to learn more, be sure to check out Robert Behnke's monumental work *Trout and Salmon of North America* Free Press, 2002.

CHAPTER 9

DOLLY VARDEN
(*Salvelinus malma*)

In the fall, mature male Dolly Varden may well be the most vividly colored, handsomely marked, and strikingly beautiful member of the char family. Dolly Varden are closely connected regionally and genetically with bull trout and Arctic char. The species can be hard to tell apart

Dolly Varden are one of the most vividly marked and colored of the Salmonidae family. When in spawning colors, their brilliance and beauty is unsurpassed.

and have often been confused, misunderstood, and disrespected by biologist and fisherman. The Dolly Varden's native range in North America is divided into a southern and northern subspecies—north and south of the Alaska Peninsula. The southern subspecies extends south only to Puget Sound in Washington State. The less common northern subspecies extends far north of Alaska.

Dolly Varden thrive best in pristine and remote cold-water streams, lakes, and coastal areas, preferring water temperature of 55 degrees Fahrenheit and lower. Their maximum size is closely related to the size of waters in which they reside. In the smallest streams the species seldom reaches two pounds, while those that live in large, food-rich waters may average four to six pounds and grow to a maximum of fifteen to twenty inches during their seven- to twelve-year life spans. The world-record Dolly was an anadromous fish weighing an incredible nineteen and a quarter pounds caught in 1998 along the Kotzebue Sound area of Alaska.

Dolly Varden mature in four to five years and spawn in September or October, usually every other year after their first spawn. I was surprised to read in Dr. Robert Behnke's *Trout and Salmon of North America* that they do not spawn adjacent

Dolly Varden will usually feed on whatever presents itself in their cold waters of limited resources. Use flies that imitate small fish, crustaceans, salmon eggs, and aquatic insects such as these, starting at the top, moving clockwise: purple articulated strip streamer, orange prawn, salmon flesh fly, glass-bead egg rig with circle hook trailer, Whitlock Double Egg and Sperm fly, October caddis pupa, Whitlock Stonefly Nymph, Clouser Parr Streamer, Whitlock Multicolored Marabou Streamer, Whitlock Matuka Sculpin.

to bull trout or Arctic char that inhabit the same regions. Thus, there is no record of them hybridizing with one another. I find this to be an amazing circumstance and an example of how well nature works when not tampered with. Anadromous Dolly Varden have a unique behavior. They enter their home rivers to spawn every other year, but in the years they do not spawn, they leave saltwater in the fall and spend the winter in lakes outside their home watersheds. During the years they are in saltwater, they stay relatively near shore and feed mostly on crustaceans and small fish.

The Dolly reportedly got its name from a colorful, fictional lady character in Charles Dickens's novel *Barnaby Rudge*. These brilliantly colored fish have rich, emerald-green backs that merge into metallic slate blue on the midsides and, on spawning males, shades of golden yellow to fiery oranges and reds. Their backs, flanks, and upper belly are profusely covered with deep-crimson spots that are haloed with gold or lavender. Pectoral, pelvic, anal, and caudal fins are starkly edged with iridescent white accented with black and pinks, oranges, or crimsons. Just describing Dollies makes this artist get goose bumps and makes me impatient to illustrate them. The only thing better is holding a fresh-caught fish for a deep (but quick) gaze.

Dolly Varden are typical opportunistic-feeding char that will eat almost anything, including insects, salmon eggs, small fish, and crustaceans and even dead salmon flesh. They will occasionally surface feed but usually prefer to feed close to the bottom and in deeper, slower water. Look for them where the run is deepest or in long, deep pools. I've found they like submerged trees, big boulders, and sharp ledge drop-offs. If you know how to tempt a big bull trout, use these same methods and artificials for Dolly Varden. The most productive flies for Dollies are those that are natural food imitators or flashy attraction streamers. That list includes egg patterns, Clousers, flesh flies, multicolored Marabou Muddlers, prawns, sculpins, Flashabou steelhead streamers, and articulated rabbit-strip streamers. Keep these flies moving slowly and close to the bottom. Dollies tend to feed best during low-

Whitlock's Multicolored Marabou Muddler. Although I created this streamer—using a large deer-hair head, rattle, and lots of marabou and flash action—to tantalize large brown trout, it became my favorite fly to catch big Dollies, bull trout, and brooks.

light levels, on overcast days or during sunrise and sunset. Though I've not done so, I have to believe the biggest ones would go for a big, black streamer on the darkest of nights.

My best experience with sizeable Dollies came while steelhead fishing the Babine River in British Columbia. The steelhead were just not cooperating, so, for variety, I began to dredge the deepest pools with a No. 5 sinking head and a size 1/0 multicolored Marabou Muddler to see what else might take my fly. To my surprise and delight, each pool I worked produced hard, positive strikes from exceptionally big Dollies, and they were wearing their autumn suits of brilliant spawning colors. They fought like demons, and I had a feeling that I'd discovered a secret mother lode of the Babine. Since that exciting encounter I've had similar Dolly action on other British Columbia salmon and steelhead rivers. Most likely a lot of British Columbia's and Alaska's steelhead and salmon rivers have big Dollies, too, but it's hard to switch over if there's a steelhead to be hooked.

Today Dolly Varden are widely respected game fish and such a lovely prize and exciting opportunity to catch on flies and lures. I think of them as I do giant brook trout—hard-fighting fish that take your breath away with their beautiful color patterns and sheer brilliance and that hang out in some of the most pristine places in the world.

Dolly Varden are very sensitive to overharvesting, reduced water quality, and disturbance in their spawning areas. To help assure their future, support TU's efforts in the Northwest to control excess timbering, mining, river damming, and uncontrolled residential and commercial watershed developments. The Dolly is worth the effort.

CHAPTER 10

LAKE TROUT
(*Salvelinus namaycush*)

Lake trout are a most significant member of North America's native salmonids because of their wide natural distribution, maximum size, and long life. Making them even more captivating to anglers and biologists are their many amazing abilities and adaptations. You might recognize lake trout by one of their many local names used across their range: gray trout, lakers, Mackinaws, lake char, and togue. This range extends across our northern border starting in Maine down into the Great Lakes to Montana then north, through most Canadian provinces and Alaska. In this huge area, lake trout reside anywhere from deep ponds to the largest lakes and larger deep rivers. Occasionally, lake trout will even inhabit the mild, brackish estuaries of these rivers.

In addition to their native range, lake trout have been stocked in many western lakes, but often not without significant impacts to native species. They have also been stocked in northern Europe, South America, and New Zealand.

Mature lake trout offer flyfishers and light-tackle anglers their best opportunity at ice-out when they feed aggressively in shallow water on schools of spring-running smelt or alewives.

Lakers have a distinctively unique body look, shape, and coloration. Their overall body and head have a grayish appearance and pearly-white or light creamy underside. A closer look reveals that they are heavily laced with numerous, irregularly shaped, pale pearlish-white or pale buttery-yellow spots on their heads, back, sides, and dorsal and caudal fins. These markings resemble chain mail to me. Their backs may be tinted with watery green, blue, or tan colors common to the waters in which they live.

Lake trout, especially males in the fall and those living in clear rivers, will usually be a bit more colorful and have moderately colored pectoral, pelvic, and anal fins similar to but not as intense as those of brook trout, Arctic char, or Dolly Varden. They have larger heads and mouths than bull trout and extra-long, heavier teeth for capturing, disabling, and swallowing other fish up to one-third to one-half their own body lengths. Another distinctive physical characteristic, which

The opossum shrimp, *Mysis relicta,* though nearly colorless and less than one-inch long, occurs over most of the natural range of lake trout and is a vital link in the lake trout's food chain, especially for deep-feeding, immature fish. It is highly adapted to thrive in very deep water—down to 900 feet or more.

allows them to swim faster, is an unusually skinny caudal peduncle that quickly expands into a very large and deeply forked tail.

When they are young, lake trout feed almost entirely on invertebrates, aquatic nymphs, leeches, and opossum shrimp. As they reach maturity, they exclusively become predators of other fish, especially smelt, alewives, sculpin, other trout, grayling, other lake trout, suckers, and whitefish. This trait has often caused near or total extermination of natural species where lake trout have been introduced. Yellowstone Lake, where illegally stocked lake trout are threatening to eradicate the native Yellowstone cutthroat, is a sad and heartbreaking example. Regulations in the park now do not allow a caught lake trout in Yellowstone Lake to be released.

I've found it curious and amazing that in most of their native lakes, deep-dwelling opossum shrimp (*Mysis*) also thrive and support the young lake trout that are driven to the deepest lake levels to find the 50-degree Fahrenheit, 4 ppm oxygen water conditions that they require. A catch-22 exists for these ideal, very-deep-water environmental conditions: they don't exist unless the water is very pure and infertile. Thus, adult lake trout living in deep water—100 to 1,200 feet—get very little to eat in the way of other fish. They grow agonizingly slow—an inch per year is not uncommon in their prime, most northern ranges, such as God's and Great Bear Lakes in northern Canada.

To compensate for this slow, short-season growth, lake trout can live much longer than other salmonids. The average in northern areas is twenty to twenty-five years, and they have actually been documented to have lived sixty-two years. That's the good news; the bad news is that trophy-sized lakers can be easily overfished in just a decade or less. Catch-and-release policies

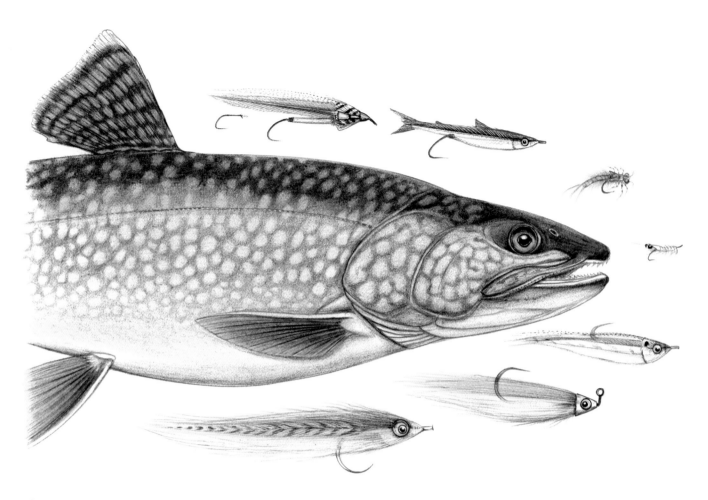

Lake trout are opportunistic feeders on opossum shrimp, burrowing mayflies, and other fish. They can be caught on flies that are imitations of these foods when they are in shallow water after ice-out and in the fall when waters again chill to 50 degrees Fahrenheit or lower.

for these extra-slow-growing trophies, where they are native, are a must to preserve them.

Most sport angling for lake trout begins with winter ice fishing. Then, at ice-out, lakers briefly forage, usually on smelt or alewives, at the surface or in lake shallows. This is the best opportunity to use light conventional tackle or fly tackle to enjoy their strong subsurface fight. Then, once the water rises above 50 degrees, they go deeper to find their comfort zone, which is usually 60 to 100 feet deep or more. Trolling with bait or lures with heavier tackle, downriggers, or wire lines reaches them

at these depths. Most of the sport is lost with this process, and trout caught this deep have a hard time surviving the depressurizing and the warmer surface temperatures.

As fall storms drop water-surface temperatures, lakers move to shallow water to feed and spawn over reefs, coarse rock bars, or along jetties or in river gravels, especially at night. I caught my first lake trout in Lake Michigan on luminous streamers in the dead of night casting along rock breakwaters in frigid late October.

In some very cold northern rivers and lakes, lakers will hold reasonably shallow at 20 to 30 feet during the summer, making them fly fishable. Usually fast (No. 5), full-sinking lines (8 weight) and large streamers take them well in these conditions. Emily and I had just such pleasurable success on six- to ten-pound lakers one July while conducting a pike fly-fishing school at Scott Lake in Saskatchewan.

The most unusual lake trout fly fishing I've experienced occurred for two years below Bull Shoals Dam in Arkansas For a short period the lake was heavily stocked with them, and, incredibly, lake trout up to four pounds could pass through the generators without lethal results. Over those two years, when two to eight generators were pushing the 52-degree water into the river, I was able to take several of these lakers on

shad streamers. They were such handsome and hard-fighting exotics.

Lake trout are unique salmonids. They grow the largest (the record is seventy-two pounds on rod and reel and a hundred and two pounds commercially caught), live the longest (60 plus years), swim the deepest (down to 1,400 feet), grow the slowest, eat the biggest mouthfuls, and are the most widely distributed. They are a special fish to be fished for, with survival and conservation always the intention.

Robert Behnke's *Trout and Salmon of North America* (Free Press, 2002) has a superb chapter on these unique salmonids. You just have to read it!

CHAPTER 11

BULL TROUT
(*Salvelinus confluentus*)

Bull trout look very much like Arctic char. They have a very limited natural range and are only found in the purest, coldest streams and rivers flowing. The common name seems to have been an attempt to characterize their predaceous, cannibalistic feeding habits or perhaps their prominent, wide head, which supports a heavy set of jaws armed with large teeth.

My first encounters with bull trout came in the early 1960s while fishing the Clark Fork River and Rock Creek in Montana. My guide warned me to be aware of an evil demon-like fish that inhabited the deeper holes of the streams—a fish that might suddenly materialize and engulf the trout on my hook! If it did, so he said, he'd shoot it and heave it into the bushes. Fortunately, the "devil" didn't show, but later I did manage to hook several small bull trout on large streamers and almost felt guilty about releasing them.

Thankfully, times have changed. In fact, it's difficult to find a current fly-fishing magazine that does not have an entire feature about or at least a brief mention of how endangered the bull trout has become and the ongoing effort to save

Big bull trout are known to be ferocious predators on other fish, especially those that are disabled or hooked.

its habitat and restrict its harvest. The fish has become so well known that, where legal to do so, anglers are now seeking out populations of bull trout to experience catching one on barbless flies.

Bull trout, in general, have the characteristic colorations and markings of char. The ones I've caught in Oregon, Montana, and Idaho during September and October somewhat resemble a hybrid form of a brook trout and a lake or brown trout. Their backs are a saucy orange-olive, sides are deep lavender with rusty-orange lower reaches, and stomachs are cream colored. They have small pale spots on their backs and pink to brilliant crimson spots on their cheeks and sides. The pectoral, pelvic, and anal fins have vivid white leading edges followed by black, then gold, and then orange. River populations are much more colorful than those that live in large lakes. All these colors ramp up in the fall, especially in males, as they prepare for their spawning activities.

Bull trout only thrive in streams and lakes where there is minimal residential development, agriculture, and timbering and where water temperatures do not exceed 60 degrees Fahrenheit. The largest bull trout are found in vast lakes and reservoirs and large rivers that run into the ocean, especially if they contain abundant populations of Kokanee salmon. Although bull trout are well known to avidly feed on other bulls, trout, and salmon, they also feed on crayfish, aquatic insects, leeches, aquatic worms, and various minnows. I once read that all you had to do to catch a huge bull trout was to find a deep hole and heave in a hook baited with a fresh chunk of beef or chicken.

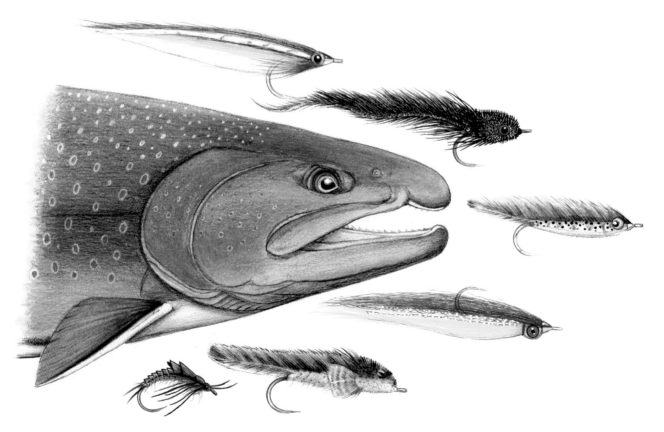

Bull trout can be consistently taken on large streamers or big nymphs. Low light level periods or high-colored water are the best conditions to entice them to these flies.

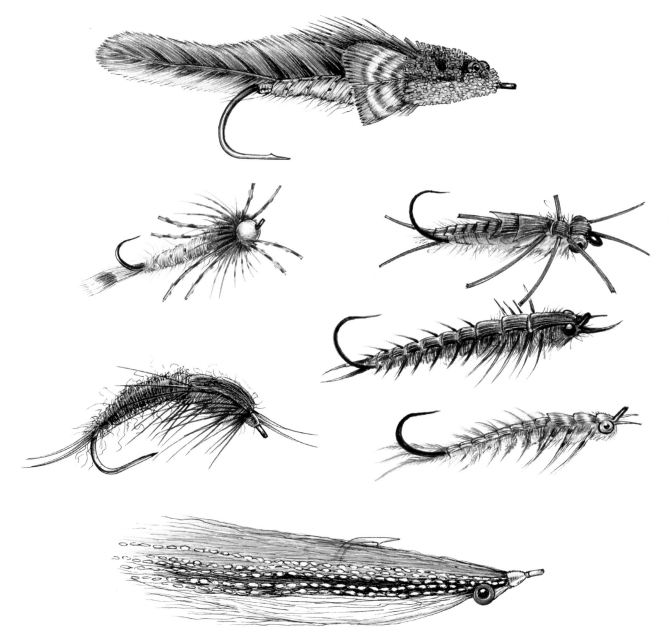

Streamers and large nymphs are the two most productive fly designs to hook into hard-fighting bull trout.

Large streamers, especially those that emit considerable low-frequency sounds and are tied with bright, colorful materials and lots of silver, gold, and red flash, seem to work best in fishing for bull trout. To tempt big bulls out of their lairs to attack trout-sized streamers, it's best to find highly colored water with temperatures ranging 45 to 55 Fahrenheit on dark, cloudy days or after dark.

Conventional anglers often use large gold, silver, or brightly colored spoons, long jerk baits, big scented swimbaits, and spinner-bucktail combinations to lure trophy bulls to their hooks.

Bull trout are usually not spectacular fighters and very seldom, if ever, leap when hooked. Nonetheless, they have a look and presence that compel anglers to focus on them. Seven- or

8-weight fly tackle and sink-tip or full-sinking, 7- or 8-weight lines are ideal for the big bulls. Light tackle and smaller streamers or large nymphs work well on small bulls when they are residing in the headwaters of their rivers.

During my lifetime I've experienced varied controversies related to bull trout, Dolly Varden, and Arctic char. Happily, these very special western North American native fish are now more clearly seen for the unique treasures they are rather than the predaceous rubbish they were branded as for so long. As humans impact nature through agriculture, timbering, mining, residential development, and fish harvesting, it's so easy to blame other creatures for the losses of the sport or food fish that humans prefer. Before we began to interrupt nature, we should recognize that animals such as wolves, birds of prey, and bull trout evolved to help keep their fellow species in balance. Thankfully, anglers and fish managers are much better informed about the importance and value of such creatures.

The bull trout's existence remains threatened by dams, overgrazing, and hybridization with nonnative brook trout. The efforts that TU and many others are making to save the bull trout and the habitat it depends upon give me great hope that nature—and all of us—have a more promising future on this place called Earth.

> Bull trout live for ten to twelve years and average about two and a half pounds. However, in large rivers and lakes that have ample food and growing season, it is common for these trout to reach the trophy size of twenty-eight to thirty-six inches. The current world record for bull trout is thirty-two pounds. It was caught in Idaho in 1949 in the huge, Kokanee salmon-laden Lake Pend Oreille.

CHAPTER 12

HYBRIDS

This chapter is devoted to salmonid species that crossbreed with other salmonid species and produce hybrid offspring. Because I am an artist, flyfisher, and trout conservationist, hybrids have always fascinated and sparked my interest. Of the salmonids—trout, salmon, char, whitefish, and grayling—the subfamily of trout, salmon, and char are most alike genetically and, when the circumstances are favorable, can produce hybrids. But, good ol' nature has been refining various species of salmonids for millions of years to create species that do not crossbreed, because hybrids generally do not contribute to the improvement or survival of the species. This "self-identity" protection is mainly accomplished by each native having separate spawning seasons, and stream nesting locations and habitats that are slightly different from one another. This works so well that it should not be surprising to learn that practically all salmonid hybrids that exist in any number are found not in nature but in hatcheries, except where man has inappropriately stocked fish that can easily hybridize with natives. The most common is when hatchery rainbows are stocked in streams that hold wild cutthroat and golden populations.

Hatchery hybridization is usually undertaken to generate income from anglers who are seeking stocked fish with exceptional vigor, growth, size, and aggressiveness, which are often common characteristics of many hybrids. In addition, many anglers (including myself) are fascinated by the unique physical traits and beauty of hybrids. Hybrids are most often produced by crossing trout with trout, char with char, or salmon with salmon, as crosses outside these groups are seldom physically or genetically possible. The only one I know of is the hybrid tiger trout, which is a cross between a male brook trout (char) and a female brown trout in carefully controlled hatchery environments. The species that lays the larger eggs must be the female for successful egg development. (Example: Brook trout eggs are on average one-third smaller than brown trout eggs, so a brown female is always crossed with a brook male for tiger trout offspring.) Only about 20 to 30 percent of the eggs actually fertilize and develop embryos, and many of these are deformed or fail to complete development. This, obviously, makes it difficult to ever produce tigers in great numbers. Tigers are only practical to stock in private waters, at considerable cost, where they are enjoyed for sport and catch and release. This hybrid does not reproduce or hybridize with other trout in a stream.

The most common and fertile hybrids are those created by a cross between rainbow trout and other westslope species, especially cutthroat, golden, and steelhead. Hatchery rainbows that are released into native cutthroat streams—usually to provide larger, harder-fighting fish that jump—can actually swiftly hybridize the natives out of existence. Another problem is that hatchery rainbows are a real mixed

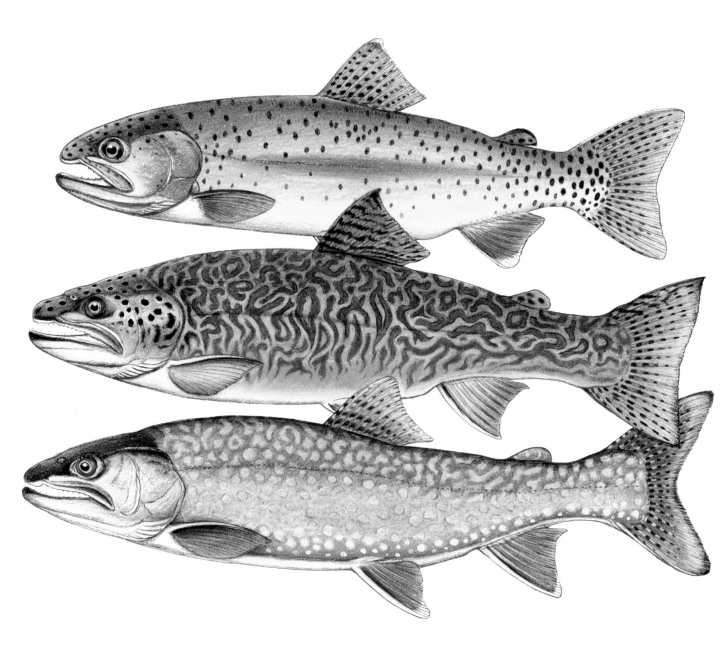

Three of the most common North American hybrid trout:

Cutbow—This is a first cross between a redband rainbow and a Yellowstone cutthroat. The hybrid looks like a rainbow with a less brilliant cut mark on its lower jaw than a cutthroat, with fewer and fainter spots and a slight gold overtone on the side and stomach.

Tiger Trout—This cross is between a female brown trout and male brook trout (a char). It is truly an eye-popping combo of tiger-like colors and vivid tiger striping. Unlike the cutbow, it is highly unlikely to occur naturally.

Splake—This is a hybrid of a female lake trout and a male brook trout. Splake grow fast, are very hardy, fight hard, and can reproduce in nature or cross back with either parent species.

bag of genetic diversity and have lost many of their natural abilities to survive in the wild, so they often struggle in the environmental conditions and diversities that the natives have successfully thrived in for millions of years. In hatcheries trout are artificially inseminated for decades, artificially fed on schedule, protected from predators and seasonal water extremes, and, because of heavy crowding in raceways, have lost the territorial instincts required for living in the wild. I find that a pretty scary way to manage a trout fishery.

The hybrids I have personal experience with are cutbows (rainbow x cutthroat), splake (brook x lake trout), tiger trout (brown x brook), steelbows (rainbow x steelhead) and brown trout x Atlantic salmon hybrids. These hybrids are all beautiful, take artificials very well, and are strong fighters. Like most salmonids, hybrids are more robust and colorful if they live outside of hatcheries in ideal water conditions and with plenty of natural foods, especially crustaceans and aquatic insects.

Cutbow—This is a first cross between a redband rainbow and a Yellowstone cutthroat. The hybrid looks like a rainbow with a less brilliant cut mark on its lower jaw than a cutthroat, with fewer and fainter spots and a slight gold overtone on the side and stomach.

Tiger Trout—This cross is between a female brown trout and male brook trout (a char). It is truly an eye-popping combo of tiger-like colors and vivid tiger striping. Unlike the cutbow, it is highly unlikely to occur naturally.

Splake—This is a hybrid of a female lake trout and a male brook trout. Splake grow fast, are very hardy, fight hard, and can reproduce in nature or cross back with either parent species.

Hybrids tend to have a higher water temperature tolerance and metabolism and so consume more food, grow faster, and are more aggressive than their parents. Several years ago I worked on a project to improve a box used to hatch salmonid eggs in the wild. The product of that research was the Whitlock-Vibert Box, an in-stream egg incubator and fry nursery that is used now to create stocks of wild trout in rivers and streams around the world. During the project, I needed to identify a species of trout that was not commonly found in streams and so could be an indicator species to prove that the Whitlock-Vibert Box had contributed to the stream trout population. The tiger trout, on paper, with its unique look and rarity was the perfect indicator fish. Part of the study included hatching tiger eggs in a big aquarium. I hatched several hundred and kept about twenty-five fry, raising them to about six to seven inches in length. They were so beautifully marked, vividly and deeply colored, intelligent, and filled-out like trout twice their size. When I released them into a small northeast Oklahoma spring creek, I became very emotional as these beautiful youngsters swam into their freedom. Later, when they were much larger, I caught two on flies, and they were awesome to experience and behold! Although tigers can be used as Whitlock-Vibert Box indicator fish, it is not recommended, as they are impractical because of their low-percentage egg development and production expense. These days every time I catch a trout, char, or salmon, I study its characteristics for expected and unexpected colors and shapes. When, on rare occasions, one appears to be a hybrid, I can't help but get a nice rush from my rare capture.

There are waters where hatchery rainbows and hybrids are a good addition, especially those that are not connected with native trout populations. But it is usually a very bad idea to stock these fish as a quick fix where native fish-

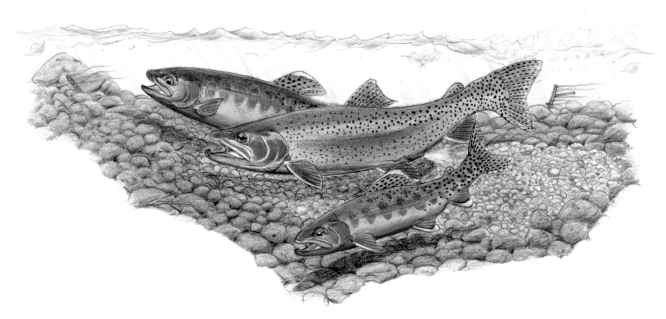

All westslope trout species can cross with hatchery redband rainbow, so their introduction into high-mountain lakes and fertile streams in order to increase catch size and sport can often backfire and cause loss of indigenous trout species. Usually larger, the redband males can easily move in on a smaller pair of native trout, chase the male aside, and pollute the gene pool.

ery habitats and populations have been abused. Hatchery trout will almost immediately break down native fish territories, causing even further loss of natives. Restoration of habitat, sometimes the removal of nonindigenous trout species and protection or reintroduction of native trout species, where possible, is often the best plan for the future of these indigenous trout, char, and salmon that have spent the last 100 million years working toward natural perfection.

CHAPTER 13

ARCTIC GRAYLING
(*Thymallus arcticus*)

If I were asked to pick a coldwater fish that could offer the most light-hearted dry-fly fishing, without hesitation I would pick the beautiful, unique Arctic grayling—especially those that are wild and abundant in the streams and rivers of Alaska and northwest Canada. Arctic grayling are adorned with a large, captivating, sail-shaped dorsal fin that is trimmed with reddish orange and painted with an aurora borealis of iridescent lavenders, pinks, and blues and rows of big, pink oval spots. This fin makes the grayling the most distinctive fish in the trout family.

The grayling's Latin name, *Thymallus*, comes from their distinctive flavor that strongly resembles the herb thyme. Being curious about that property, I decided to try one. To me it tasted like a combination of thyme and whitefish.

I always see grayling as having expressive eyes. These eyes are big and golden and set into

Arctic grayling often, as if to display the incredible aurora borealis of colors and sleek shape of their dorsal fin, make water-clearing leaps to pounce on surface-hovering insects.

a petite head. The scales are a shimmering purple, pink, and gold and are much larger than other trout. The body is sleek with a strong, richly colored, deep-blue and pink, deeply forked tail. The oversized, multihued pelvic fins seem to provide a perfect counterbalance to that splendid dorsal fin. The males have the larger dorsal fin and most vivid colors. To this artist they look like a successful hybrid of a pacific sailfish, rainbow trout, and Rocky Mountain whitefish.

The North American Arctic grayling's range extends from most of Alaska through northwest and northcentral Canada and south to an isolated population in Montana and stocked populations in a number of ponds and lakes in adjacent Rocky Mountain states. Once there even existed a population in Michigan that is now extinct. Over this range they are most abundant and largest in waters that are very cold, have little fishing pressure, are pristine, and have low saline and silt contents.

Grayling congregate in small schools or pods. In Montana, I've often encountered them among groups of Rocky Mountain whitefish. They average eight to twelve inches but exceed that in some Canadian and Alaskan waters where three- to four-pound fish are trophies, but also rare. The current world record is five pounds fifteen ounces, taken from a river at Great Bear Lake in Canada.

Similar to whitefish, grayling are more prolific spawners than trout or char by a factor of two or three and do not make nests or redds, but instead scatter their numerous small eggs over coarse-gravel river bottoms. The eggs filter down

Because Arctic Grayling have relatively small mouths and prefer aquatic and terrestrial insects, small, dark, or colorful dry flies, emergers, wet flies, and nymphs work most consistently to catch them.

into the gravel crevices, incubate, and hatch in a shorter time period than trout eggs.

Although grayling do eat trout and salmon eggs and small fish at times, what they most prefer are aquatic and terrestrial insects. Small, dark or bright-colored nymphs, soft hackles, and dry flies are incredibly effective artificials for grayling. They mainly focus on surface feeding, and this strong preference makes them a supreme dry-fly fishing experience. They have an endless rise repertoire, from the most subtle tip-and-sip to frequent and flamboyant, double-their-length, up-and-down flying vaults that enable them to pounce down on a surface-hovering or floating insect.

The rise impression of the Arctic "sailfish" seems carefree and joyful and is so darn amusing and exciting to experience that we can't keep from laughing with them. If that were not enough, they always seem to be in an opportunistic mood to rise to any small dry fly. Often, in their utter exuberance, they will miss the fly but will continue rising and jumping at it until they get it.

There have been times in Alaska and Saskatchewan, using a 10-foot, 3- or 4-weight rod and floating line, when I've skated two or three dry flies over a surfacing grayling and suddenly had three or four fish bounding up and down on my skittering flies. Talk about sheer joy—that's it! It's entirely possible to connect with two or three grayling at the same time using dropper wet flies, soft hackles, or dry flies.

Grayling have small, tender mouths, and to release them unharmed it's best to use very small, barbless flies, usually sizes 14 to 20. I also prefer to use softer-action rods to assist in preventing mouth damage and break offs. Catch-and-release nets are a must for landing to prevent damage to their lovely, fragile fins.

I caught my first graylings on the upper Big Hole River in Montana between Jackson and the Continental Divide. They were delightfully beautiful but also very small. Later I took a few

Grayling seem almost childlike with carefree enthusiasm as they encounter flying adult aquatic insects or the dry flies that imitate them.

larger ones tubing in Yellowstone Park's Grebe Lake. A good friend of mine, Dick Storts, while fishing the upper Madison River with spinning tackle, hooked and landed a twenty-inch, three-pound grayling. Sometime later I learned that grayling had never been known to get that big there and were actually supposed to be extinct in that entire area. That fish remains a mystery to me. But it was on Bristol Bay's Agulapak River in Alaska where I had my most spectacular dry-fly, grayling fishing experience, catching numerous fifteen- to nineteen-inch sailfins. About half of those "monsters" were such a deep, deep purple that I can still see them clearly in my mind.

Graylings get my vote for the most fun and most beautiful cold-water fish you can catch on a dry fly. They fight like champs, jump and leap, and never fail to reward with their unique loveliness and endless energy and spunk. Even in my hand or net, they seem to be carefree and smiling as I release them. But then, I have a great imagination!

CHAPTER 14

MOUNTAIN WHITEFISH
(*Prosopium williamsoni*)

The mouth structure of mountain whitefish is perfect for capturing small, slow-moving food forms on stream bottoms; however, when a significant aquatic emergence occurs or large numbers of small, floating spent insects, such as flying ants, mayflies, and midges are present, they will feed up the water column and on the surface.

Last August I watched a wading guide on the Snake River land a fine-sized fish for my fishing friend. He quickly unhooked it, put it behind his back, and dropped it into the water . . . before I had a chance to photograph it. I asked what it was, and in a low voice he said, "Whitefish." At least he didn't launch it into the streamside growth like I've seen many folks do over the years.

Although mountain whitefish are maligned by many fly anglers, they are special and unique trout/grayling-like fish that are keen fly-fishing sport when approached with tiny flies, light rods, and the skill to use the lightest of tippets (even up to 8X). They are a valuable resource as food for trout and other predators. My whitefish memories are of many pleasant experiences that span my life as a flyfisher. From my first beginner trips to the Yellowstone River at age sixteen, to season-after-season catch encounters, to delicious stream-side lunches of batter-fried filets, to watching my students' joy as they developed new skills with nymphs and dry flies on a big school of twelve-to-sixteen-inch whites, and to my joy of reunion with them not long ago on the Henry's Fork and Madison Rivers.

Light-tackle anglers might compare whitefish in cold waters to bluegills in warm water—always available and plentiful to find and catch, regardless of our age, income, and tackle quality. And you can enjoy a meal of them without guilt.

One September in the late 1980s, I spent a wonderful month out West in my VW camper detoxing from work stress by canoeing, fly fishing, and bird hunting on the Yellowstone and Bighorn Rivers—alone except for my wonderful German shorthair, Koko. Every other day, between bird meals, we'd share campfire-grilled or pan-fried whitefish, and neither of us ever left a bite of those beautiful, extra-firm, pearl-white filets on our plates.

Mountain whitefish are indigenous to rivers and lakes of northwest North America, from the Great Basin and Green River basin north to the Columbia and Fraser River basins, on north to the Mackenzie River basin of Canada. Curiously, the mountain whitefish is also a native of streams of the east-flowing Missouri River drainage, including the Yellowstone below the Park falls. In their native waters, mountain whitefish average about nine to twelve inches but will often grow to eighteen inches and can exceed two to three pounds within seven or eight years. At three or four years old, they mature and spawn in mid- to late fall, and, instead of constructing redds as trout do, they deposit and fertilize eggs over a wide section of stream or lake shoal water like

grayling. They lay around 5,000 grayling-size 3mm eggs per female pound.

All whitefish have very small, tender mouths with a weak, boneless mandible lower jaw that is indicative of capturing and eating small invertebrates, especially on or near the bottom in streams. They will, however, feed actively on the surface, much like trout and grayling, when there is a significant emergence or spinner fall of aquatic insects such as blue-winged olives (BWOs), tricos, or flying ants. Midges and BWOs often work well all winter!

You can find (or avoid) whitefish, in small pods to very large schools, by recognizing their preferred holding water, which is usually in midstream sections that are deep and slow and have dense, coarse weed, rock, or wood structure. For those who do not wish to catch these interesting fish, simply use a quick hook set or apply lots of rod pressure to free the fly from their small and very tender mouths . . . leaving more for me! Mountain whitefish can tolerate higher water temperatures than trout and will feed actively all winter long, making them a fish that is almost always available in the waters of their native ranges. Chances are that these whitefish will survive much better in their streams than trout will as climate changes occur.

Although mountain whitefish are not closely related to Arctic grayling, I've always seen them as grayling without the big dorsal fin. In fact, in the 1950s–1970s, I often took grayling and whitefish from the same pods of surface feeders, or in nymphing runs on the Big Hole and Madison inside Yellowstone Park. Maybe they thought they were mixing with kinfolk. Mountain whitefish are actually in the trout family and have a similar but more rounded form than trout as well as a comparable soft-rayed adipose fin, only a bit larger. To me, they are shaped much more like a bonefish crossed with a grayling than a trout, and their very firm bodies are typical of extra strong and fast game fish. They have a distinctive, pointed nose with a wimpy little toothless lower jaw, much like a bonefish, and they seem to be perpetually smiling. As in trout, young whitefish also have parr markings. Their eyes are big and bright yellow with a slightly elongated black pupil that gives them a distinctively excited, almost staring expression. Mountain whitefish are anything but white in color and have an olive-brown back, bluish golden-brown sides, a pearly French-gray underside, large spotless scales, and an eye-catching tint of rouge on their gill plates. This red comes partly from their red gill filaments that show through their transparent gill covers. I suspect one reason for their name is from their pearl-white flesh.

Although mountain whitefish have not suffered the near extinction of many lake whitefish populations—especially in the Midwest and eastern lakes due to their delicious flavor and commercial netting—I'm concerned by what I've heard and experienced lately. Because of their historical abundance, competition for trout space and forage, lack of aerial displays when hooked, and lack of spots, there have been almost no restrictions of seasons and sizes, methods, and numbers of mountain whitefish harvested. Because they are heavily harvested by winter anglers, mature fish are at all-time lows in too many rivers. Despite what some think of whitefish, this is serious news for the species, as they are important forage for the entire ecosystem where they evolved—just as salmon are to British Columbian and Alaskan ecosystems. Their disappearance in our famous trout rivers means slower trout growth rates, more trout cannibalism on their own, and lower fishing quality. True natives of most western waters, these remarkable fish

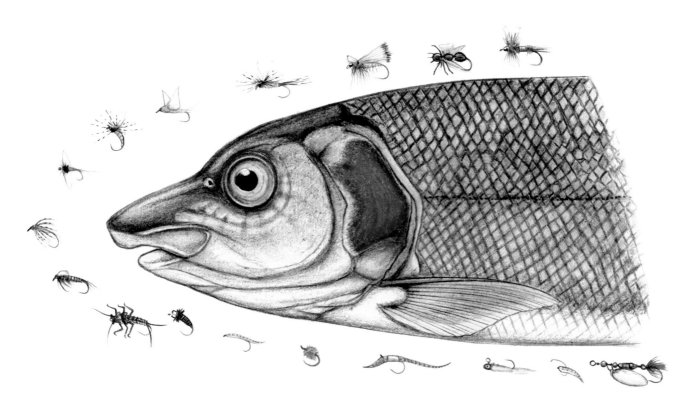

Mountain whitefish have a small, toothless mouth design and prefer to feed on small invertebrates; therefore, fly sizes 12 to 24 are the most effective.

deserve the same protection afforded trout in order to preserve and conserve their populations.

Speaking of quality, there is a growing group of nonconformist guides, flyfishers, tenkara fishers, and thread liners focusing on trophy whitefish. They all say that to catch a three-pound whitefish requires more skill than taking a trophy trout. The largest whitefish are most consistently landed when using 7X to 8X tippet and size 20 to 26 hooks, not because they won't take heavier stuff, but because their mouths are so tender and they fight so doggedly long, and we don't tend to muscle any fish on 7X and 8X tippet and size 20 or smaller flies. Most trophies that I've personally encountered have been in larger rivers where they enter lakes, such as the Madison River near Hebgen Lake and Quake Lake.

I hope this helps open your eyes a little more to the special nature of mountain whitefish. They are one neat game fish with which you can sharply hone your light-tackle dry-fly, nymph, and wet-fly fishing skills, and they are a great way to enthuse a beginner. Give them a try next time you're out West and catch them intentionally!

CHAPTER 15

STEELHEAD
(*Oncorhynchus mykiss irideus*)

Migratory Pacific coastal rainbow trout from Southern California to the Gulf of Alaska are called steelhead. These great trout are truly remarkable in size, color, and life cycles. They are sprinting, leaping, and tireless sport fish and, in my opinion, are rivaled only by the magnificent Atlantic salmon.

In my lifetime, I've seen steelheading become amazingly popular with flyfishers. That, in turn, has elevated these splendid fish in our art, literature, photography, and fly tying into true and mystical trophy fish. The capture of a mature, wild steelhead on a fly is always a very special event to me, as it is with most flyfishers that I've

During their upstream journey, steelhead undergo drastic color changes—gradually replacing their steely-chrome sides and pewter back-color with vivid chroma of green, red, and white and irregular, inky-black spots on their backs and fins.

shared fishing experiences with. You'll seldom read how many steelhead are lost in a day's fishing, while landing one out of every three or four that are hooked is an excellent average.

Steelhead begin their lives much like other rainbow trout—born from eggs deposited in carefully chosen gravels in headwater reaches of streams during the spring. The fry and parr basically look identical to immature resident, nonmigratory rainbows. After two or three years of life as stream trout, steelhead begin to move downstream and transform in color from the typical heavily spotted, green-backed, pink-sided, bronze-and-white-stomached rainbow trout to nearly colorless, spotless, chrome-finished smolts. These first-time migrants swim out into the expanses of the Pacific Ocean or into the Great Lakes for steelhead that have been transplanted there.

These transformed beauties live a sea life, feeding heavily and growing as much as an inch a month for three or more years. Then those that survive sea lions, giant squid, sharks, tuna, humans, and other predators return to their home rivers as long, sleek, silver torpedoes, affectionately called "chromers." They come back to mate and lay their eggs, not to feed. These spawning runs can occur one, two, or three times during a season. Summer, fall, and winter runs of fish move up the river at various rates, but they all spawn in the following spring. The surviving kelts (spawners) swim back to the sea to feed and further develop. They will eventually return for a second and, occasionally, a third spawning run. Steelhead that postpone their first spawning run for two or three years obtain outlandish weights and lengths.

During their upstream river journey, steelhead undergo drastic color changes—gradually replacing their steely-chrome sides and pewter back-color with a vivid green, red, and white and irregular, inky-black spots on their backs, sides, and fins. The males develop a full fluorescent hue of crimson red, purple, and lavender on

Steelhead are magnificent leapers when hooked and epitomize the definition of the perfect fish for sport angling.

Summer- and fall-run steelhead, especially those that are chrome-colored, fresh from the sea, and holding in shallow tail outs, will rise to a fly that is precisely waked by their heads.

their sides, gill plates, and lower fins. It's hard to decide which phase, chrome or chroma, is the most beautiful.

Compared to the shape of nonmigratory rainbow, the body of the steelhead is longer and sleeker. Their scales seem larger and to me resemble polished-silver chain mail. Their heads seem smaller and their tails larger, with an almost straight or square edge. The dorsal, adipose, pectoral, pelvic, and anal fins are smaller and more streamlined than those of resident, nonmigratory rainbows. It's obvious that sea life provides the diet, exercise, and speed from predator avoidance that it takes to make them true super trout. Few obstacles can detain them from completing their upstream

journey to find the spawning grounds where they originated, as any steelhead flyfisher can tell you.

I find it incredible that steelhead reenter freshwater so heavily fortified with food stores that they do not have to eat to maintain their strength and energy until spawning occurs, even if that is a six- to nine-month waiting period. However, some do occasionally eat. They can be enticed to take baits, lures, and flies, especially those that are fished at the correct depths or moving on the surface in ways that stimulate their instinctive predatory nature. Because steelhead have no particular need to eat when they move upriver to spawn, usually only a low percentage can be tempted to take flies. Those flies

Most steelhead flies are subsurface swimmers that have lots of water movement and are tied with highly visible colors to attract or excite these nonfeeding prespawners into striking.

From left to right, top to bottom: Skykomish Sunrise, Bright Ember Mari-Boo, Double Egg Sperm Fly, Orange Heron Spey Wet Fly, Popsicle, Babine Burgundy Bunny, Prawn fly, String Leech.

Popular steelhead dry flies. Left to right: Fin's Steelhead Skater, Muddler Minnow, Waller Waker, Royal Wulff, October Skater.

that imitate salmon eggs, nymphs, and prawn, drifted naturally and deep, can take fish consistently. But today, fishing with floating lines and attractor wet and surface-waking flies, often on long, double-handed spey rods, is the most popular method to catch them on flies. This requires precise down and across-stream speed and motion techniques to attract, excite, and trigger a positive rise to take a fly that they, essentially, don't need to eat. Flyfishers, like myself, who fish mainly for resident, feeding trout, can have quite a long and fishless learning curve before success begins in earnest. Even then, one steelhead a day is considered excellent!

It often requires fishing attractors for hundreds (or even thousands) of casts to finally stimulate just one steelhead into rising to a fly. But, when that happens, you'll most likely be connected to the largest, hardest-fighting, most beautiful trout you've ever caught. A fly-hooked steelhead can cover more air and water space simultaneously in more directions and more quickly than any other freshwater game fish I've caught. They seem to be in and out of both ends of a pool at the same time! So, when you hook your steelhead, your steelhead will most likely hook you, too!

I had my first experiences fly fishing for summer/fall-run steelhead in the 1970s. At that

time, I had caught Atlantic salmon on floating lines and floating flies. I saw so many parallels between Atlantic salmon and steelhead, but most steelhead fishing was done with sinking lines and sinking flies. Yet, as I fished for them with this method, I often noticed steelhead making very definite surface rises.

One afternoon, while drinking a cup of hot coffee on the bank of a Babine River pool, I saw a very large steelhead rise to what looked like a small, colorful floating maple leaf. I put down the coffee, changed to a floating line, and found a muddler minnow in my fly box. I tied it on, dressed it good with floatant, and cast above the second rise of that big steelhead. As the fly floated over the steelhead's midriver lie for the third time, the big beauty rose, waked, and squarely took the muddler. I hooked it! This sleek silver-and-crimson torpedo did its steelhead thing all over the pool and then, after an exciting tail walk, ejected the muddler. It all happened so quickly, I wasn't sure that I hadn't imagined it. I told my fishing companions back at the lodge that evening, but no one seemed to really believe me.

About two years later, I landed an eight-pound hen on the North Umpqua on a big hair-wing October caddis. As the fly floated over her, she responded just like an Atlantic salmon would to a waking dry fly! This time, my friend Dennis Black was there to witness it. After that October afternoon, I believe a new era of surface fishing for steelhead began.

For much more information on steelhead, I recommend reading these excellent books:

A Steelheader's Way: Principles, Tactics, and Techniques, by Lani Waller. Headwater Books (2012).

Steelhead Fly Fishing, by Trey Combs. Lyons Press (1991).

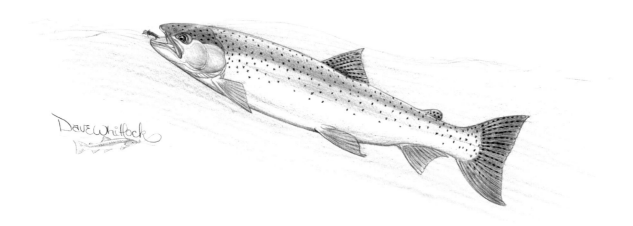

CHAPTER 16

ATLANTIC SALMON
(Salmo salar)

*S*almo salar: the name alone has a poetic beauty, even for those who have never seen one. To those of us who have come eye-to-eye with or hooked one of these splendid fish on a fly, the name wells up some very deep emotions. The wild Atlantic salmon, often called the king of game fish, is one magnificent creature. The opportunities I've had to watch them rocketing up and over waterfalls or torpedoing below the surface of a lovely stream, rising to one of my flies or recreating them on canvas, are among the most vivid memories of my life. To me they are the perfect fish in form, size, beauty, strength, elegance, and lifestyle. Every inch of their beautiful form, from their bullet-shaped nose to their perfect laminar-flow body proportions to their broad, powerful tails, allows them to explosively accelerate and leap to heart-stopping heights.

Because of their elegant form, speed, enduring stamina, and amazing leaping ability, Atlantic salmon are often called the king of game fish. Tempting one to rise to a fly can be a definitive cold-water angling experience.

Atlantic salmon are androgynous fish with a home range in the North Atlantic from the most northeastern United States to Canada and then eastward across the Atlantic to Iceland, the British Isles, and Europe to Russia. There are two forms—sea run and landlocked. I'll discuss the landlocks in the next chapter.

Sea-run Atlantic salmon have a similar life cycle to Pacific salmon and steelhead, but unlike Pacific salmon, they do not die after spawning. When mature salmon enter their pristine home rivers to spawn, they are sheathed in sterling silver, packed solid with deep, reddish-orange muscle, and are supercharged with the ocean's vitality.

They enter with the tides in several groups from April to July, each group stimulated by the river level of their home waters. Their journey takes them miles upstream through long pools, runs, riffles, rapids, and boiling waterfalls, where they pause now and then for minutes, hours, or sometimes days before continuing to the tributaries where they were born. By October or November they pair, mate, and deposit their eggs in the protective gravels of their natal streams.

Each day they are in the river, their colors and spots change to resemble their close kin, the brown trout—*Salmo trutta*. After spawning, the mature salmon are half-starved, lean, and

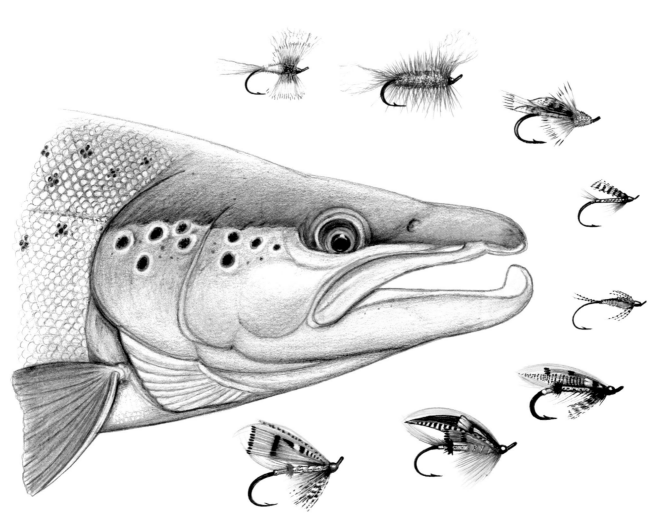

Atlantic Salmon do not feed after they enter freshwater rivers to spawn but will rise to a tempting assortment of flies skillfully presented and fished.

leaden-colored from their months of fasting and spawning. Now called kelts, they remain nearly dormant until early spring thaw, when rising runoff from snow and rains begin to sweep them back to the Atlantic, triggering their digestive systems to turn on. Hordes of spring-spawning smelt, running up the river, provide them their first replenishing meals in months. Soon afterward, for those that make it back to tidewater, the sea's richness begins to reverse the degenerative effects of their spawning cycle. The largest salmon are most often repeat spawners, but it's estimated that only about 10 percent of Atlantic salmon survive their first run and return life in the ocean to make a second. And very, very few survive long enough for a third run.

Salmon salar are seldom taken for sport in salt water and are mainly fished for as they progress upstream before they spawn. To my knowledge, all US Atlantic salmon rivers are now closed to fishing because our native wild salmon are hovering close to extinction in all of them. Canadian rivers are less degraded, and most are restricted to fly fishing only, some just catch and release.

These incredible fish do not eat once they leave the oceans to spawn, and so tempting them to rise to an artificial fly is one of the most challenging endeavors in all of angling. The process is both fascinating and frustrating. Only one or two salmon in a pool might take a fly on any given day—or maybe none. Taking one on a fly becomes a long, calculated ritual of showing each salmon what you have in your fly box of shapes, sizes, colors, and actions. From parr to the adults you cast over, salmon are predators of insects, fishes, squid, crabs, shrimp, eels, and so on. It's up to the angler to trigger the dormant feeding instinct to get them to capture an object that is moving through their space. This scenario is so infectious that one can easily devote an entire day trying to raise one particular salmon—or a lifetime and small fortune trying to capture just a few of these remarkable sky leapers.

Here's a personal experience that might help someone who has not fished for Atlantic salmon to understand what it's all about.

One June morning I began fishing a big pool just below a highway bridge on the St. John River a mile above tidewater on the Gaspé Peninsula in Quebec. I was using a big hair-wing dry fly. On about the twentieth cast, a beautiful eighteen- to twenty-pound, chrome-plated hen fish, just out of the sea, rose up through the six or eight feet of transparent, turquoise flow and drifted for a couple of feet, right below my fly, no more than two or three inches from it, while my heart almost stopped beating. Then she suddenly dove and disappeared. That began a three-hour scenario between her and me of "show me what else you have in your fly box" rises and rejections. She'd flip a dry fly with her nose, swirl beneath the next or drown it with her tail, and she would have no part of a wet fly. Several times she actually barrel rolled as she swam back to her hiding position. She was having sport with my dry flies—and perhaps me—as I know we made eye contact during many of the rises she made. Finally, nearly out of choices, I tied on an unlikely option—a Lee Wulff molded-plastic body, yellow, stonefly adult. On the first drift over her position, her great form materialized under the fly, drifted with it for several feet, vanished, and then suddenly reappeared to snatch the fly between her jaws.

As it had been for the previous three hours, it continued to be all her show. Feeling the hook, she jetted away and then began leaping over every section of the eighty-yard pool. It almost seemed like there were two salmon jumping at both ends of the pool at the same time! It was surrealistic.

When hooked on a fly, Atlantic salmon make amazing leaps that seem to defy gravity.

Suddenly, without warning, she dashed upstream out of the pool and under a bridge, circled a piling, and bolted down in front of me, where she leaped once more and broke off the fly in her jaw. Game over. I figure we were both winners, though, and no one could have ever had a more exciting three hours of fishing sport than that Atlantic lady presented to me.

Adding up the Atlantic salmon's virtues—flawless form and beauty, amazing strength and speed, their moodiness, the lovely places in the world where they live, the gorgeous flies used to lure them, and the thrill of connecting with one, if even for a moment—it's easy to understand why flyfishers who experience these fish honor them as king of the game fishes.

CHAPTER 17

LANDLOCKED SALMON
(Salmo salar sebago)

The elegant landlocked salmon (*Salmo salar sebago*), one of my most favorite fish, is a direct descendant of Atlantic salmon (*Salmo salar*). But unlike Atlantic salmon, which spend their life in both fresh and salt water, landlocks never return to the ocean and instead live their entire lives in deep, cold, freshwater lakes and the major river tributaries of these lakes. They become landlocked through various historic geological and climatic events, or through stocking by man. Fortunately, they have retained the perfect form, beauty, speed, and leaping ability of their sea-run brethren. Though smaller than the typical Atlantic salmon, landlocks are a dream fish for trout anglers because they react like trout on steroids. In the northeastern areas of the United States and Canada, they are also more affordable, numerous, and accessible for flyfishers than are Atlantic salmon.

In the lower 48 states, landlocks were native to Maine's Lake Sebago but are now stocked in over 300 waters in Maine and widely in several other extreme northeastern states. Abundant wild populations of Canadian landlocks, called

Landlocked salmon are smaller than their sea-run ancestors and are fantastic leapers and hard, fast, and long-winded fighters when hooked on small flies and light tackle.

ouananiche, exist in Quebec, Labrador, and Newfoundland lakes and their tributaries. For a new destination experience, plan a trip to these provinces for an ultimate wild medley of giant brook trout and high-flying landlocked salmon.

The best blue-ribbon, landlocked fishing is found in large, deep, cold, acid-free, unpolluted, nutrient-rich lakes that have dense populations of forage fish—especially smelt—and abundant summer hatches of aquatic insects. The average size of landlocks is fourteen to twenty-two inches, and fish over five or six pounds are rare. Occasionally, I have seen and hooked fish that might exceed nine or ten pounds. I caught a surprise twelve-pounder in Michigan's Père Marquette River one summer while fly fishing for brown trout. The extraordinary size, I was told, was the result of landlocks that were experimentally stocked in Lake Michigan, where the fish found unlimited hordes of alewives to feed on. The world record forty-five-pound landlock came from a large form found in Lake Vättern Sweden.

My first experience with landlocks was in the mid-'70s at a Berkley tackle representatives meeting on Grand Lake Stream in Maine. On a frigid day in late April, I went out with a guide and caught several landlocked salmon by trolling a fly tipped with a smelt in the wake of his Grand Lake Streamer canoe. The next day I managed to hook three or four dark, skinny, almost lifeless kelts below the dam on streamer flies and a sinking line. Both experiences were not the kind that would make me want to fish for landlocks again.

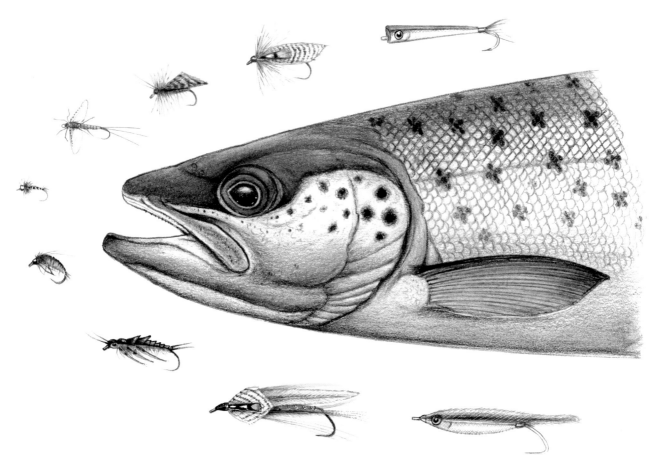

Landlocked salmon feed from top to bottom on a wide variety of small fish and insects.

But in 1981, after I established and began directing the L.L. Bean fly-fishing schools in Maine, I fished the Rapid River, upper Penobscot, and Grand Lake Stream in June and July. My encounters with the prime, well-fed landlocked salmon in these rivers were a 180-degree shift from my previous experience.

I fished to landlocks selectively feeding on nymphs, pupae, duns, and spinners using 4- and 5-weight rods. These salmon were absolutely amazing in their selectivity, and when finally hooked, they entertained me with countless vaults, flashing tail walks, and torpedo-speed runs! I was suddenly hooked on landlocks. I couldn't help wondering where these wonderful fish had been all my life.

Landlocks, like their sea-run relatives, have a beautiful, flawless body design and are richly tattooed with large, inky spots that often look like the letter *x*. Body colors range from bright,

Seasons of Salar Sebago.

Winter—Kelts are lean and a dull chrome-pewter color.

Spring—Salmon that remain in rivers after winter grow robust and brightly colored and marked by feeding on smelt and aquatic and terrestrial insects.

Summer—Salmon that return to their lake habitat become heavier and brightly chrome plated.

Fall—From September to November, landlocks move up into their rivers to spawn. They transform into a rich chroma of colors and heavy spotting, similar to that of their brown trout relatives.

polished chrome to intense burnt orange, yellow, and olive hues with a pattern of vivid black and rusty red spots. These beauties swim fast, jump really high, and can often be almost impossibly selective when feeding on black flies and midges, mayfly spinner falls, emerging midges, or caddis hatches. Through the summer the biggest ones cannot resist a deep-drifted, size 6 or 4 stonefly nymph or dragonfly nymph. One morning on Maine's Rapid River, I hooked three landlocks of sea-run proportions fishing just that way.

A good example of landlocked salmon's ultraselectivity happened to me one June in the '80s when I was wade fishing the Rapid River one early morning during a mayfly spinner fall. I found a group of landlocks steadily rising to these spinners. My spinner imitation got numerous looks and just as numerous refusals. Suddenly a twisted 6X tippet made my spinner flip over several times. That did it! A wonderful eighteen-incher immediately took the "perfectly" animated fly. I tried again, several times, but could never get the tippet to twist and move in just that way again—and the fish all looked the other way!

The best match-the-hatch wade fishing occurs after the spring smelt runs in larger streams that maintain cold flows all summer, especially the tailwater sections below power dams like the one on the upper Penobscot. If the stream warms to above 65 to 72 degrees Fahrenheit, most land-locks will move downstream into the cold depths of lakes, returning in the fall to spawn in October or November, after the rivers cool again. Those few that stay in the warmer rivers shouldn't be fished for due to the stressful conditions. Although landlocks rise beautifully to aquatic insects, most often they are caught while casting streamers on rivers during the early spring smelt runs, by trolling in lakes, or by using attractor streamers during fall spawning runs.

My most unusual landlocked encounter took place one early summer on the upper St. Croix River in Maine. I was bugging for smallmouth and chain pickerel along a boulder-strewn run using a silver, surface-skipping, three-inch-long balsa pencil popper when a twenty-inch landlock jumped the bug and then leaped skyward so high it killed itself colliding with a big, exposed, mid-stream rock on its descent from its six-foot-high leap. I was simultaneously brokenhearted and utterly amazed.

If you find the opportunity to catch one of nature's best creatures while wading in a clear, cold, Northeastern stream—while matching a hatch using light rods and fine tippets—you'll surely, like myself, want to adopt them and take them with you to live in your home trout streams. Landlocked salmon are so beautiful, so fast, and leap so high that they are truly everything a trout angler could wish for.

CHAPTER 18

THE PACIFIC SALMON

My depiction of the males of the five Pacific salmon at the prime peak of their spawning colors. From top to bottom: chum, coho, sockeye, pink, king.

Five species of true Pacific salmon exist in North American waters: Chinook (king); coho; sockeye; chum; and pink. There are no recognized subspecies or hybrids because each species is so uniquely specific in their life cycles and habitats. But a few things are the same. They are all anadromous, meaning each of these species begins life in a freshwater stream and, after a time, swims downstream and out into the ocean to grow and mature. When they are healthy and old enough to spawn, they are driven by their instincts to travel back to their freshwater birthplace and spawn in the same spot, if they can—and then they die. The miraculous bounty of nutrients offered each year by this life cycle makes it possible for the entire ecosystem to survive these harsh, cold regions of the world.

The startling transformation that salmon go through as they begin their epic run to their spawning grounds almost defies believing. As the members of each species enter their rivers from the ocean, they all have shiny, pewter-colored backs and silvery, almost colorless, sides. All are very similar in body shape, if not in size. After

only a few hours to days in freshwater, their hormones begin to alter their shapes and colors dramatically, especially the males. By the end of their spawned-out life, they are barely recognizable as the same fish that began the journey. Death within a few short hours or days mercifully overtakes their spent and worn forms, and, within weeks, their gaunt bodies disappear into the food chain of their home streams. It's easy to feel a sense of sadness or loss for these remarkable salmon, but the gravels beneath their decaying forms contain millions of bright, reddish-orange eggs that will soon create another generation of Pacific salmon to continue their species' timeless legacy.

Brightly colorful flies can be used to induce salmon entering fresh water to strike, even though they are not able to actually feed.

CHAPTER 19

KING, OR CHINOOK, SALMON
(Oncorhynchus tshawytscha)

The Chinook salmon is commonly called king salmon because of its giant size, spectacular strength, and awesome endurance. They are also called black-mouth salmon because their mouth tissue is dark pewter in color. Adult kings average twenty-five pounds and often reach forty to fifty pounds. To most trout flyfishers, the sight of a fifty-pound king salmon is almost surreal. The official all-tackle world record is 97.5 pounds caught in Alaska in 1985, and the record commercial-caught is 126 pounds, also in Alaska. The Siberian huchen (tai-men) is the only salmonid that has been reported to exceed the king salmon in weight.

In North America, the king salmon ranges wild in the Pacific region from California to Alaska and the Yukon. Kings comprise about 10 percent of the total number of all Pacific region salmon. Chinook have also been successfully introduced to the Great Lakes but are mostly

As Chinooks begin their spawning journey, their body color and shape alters daily from bright chromes to golds, oranges, rusty reds, and finally to dark pewter and dull rusty maroons. The male makes the most drastic transformation.

hatchery stocked as parr or smolts. The anadromous kings live in the Pacific Ocean for three to five years before they seek out their freshwater home streams—usually large river systems—to spawn and then to die almost precisely where they were born. There seems to be no limit to the distance kings will swim up river to reproduce—even as far as 2,000 miles.

I've personally witnessed this epic voyage, and it is an emotional and humbling experience. Chinooks usually enter their freshwater rivers on their one and only spawning run in spring and must traverse through, over, and past a complicated gauntlet of extreme rapids, waterfalls, man-made structures, predators, and fishermen. The survivors of the journey lay and fertilize 3,000 to 6,000, marble-sized eggs (7 mm) and deposit them in coarse gravel nests (redds) exactly at the same spot, when possible, where they were born.

After about three months, the salmon fry emerge from the redds and begin the next generation's life cycle. Feeding ravenously day and night on nearly anything that moves including aquatic insects, crustaceans, and trout eggs, Chinook parr develop into seaworthy smolts and return to the ocean within six months to two years, depending on the stream fertility, water temperatures, and lengths of their home waters.

I once hatched several hundred eggs of kings, coho, steelhead, Atlantic salmon, rainbow, and brown trout as part of my development of the Whitlock-Vibert Box. I placed the fry into a very large aquarium that was equipped to create water currents and fed them live brine shrimp in order

Chinook are voracious sea feeders on other fish, crab, shrimp, and squid. However, once they enter freshwater to spawn, they cannot eat but do continue to strike lures and flies that simulate their once-favorite foods or those that invade their space.

to continue to study their behaviors. After about ninety days, the only fry left in the tank were the kings. They had grown the fastest and had eaten every other salmon and trout in the tank, then they began to eat one another! In the end, only a few of the most robust and aggressive king parr survived. It was an incredible testimony to the superiority of their size, aggression, and appetite. I've also witnessed this ferocious behavior in king smolts in Lake Michigan streams as I trout fished during their downstream migration to the Great Lakes inland seas.

This aggression continues and amplifies as Chinooks live and grow in the ocean for the next three to five years, feeding on forage fish, crustaceans, and squid. When they finally return to their freshwater home streams, they are packed with hard, tempered muscles and are as polished and silver as chrome. Most sport fishing occurs when they are still fresh from the sea and in the lower sections of the rivers. As soon as they start their swim upstream, they stop feeding but will attack objects such as flies, lures, and fish that enter their territory, even killing trout that attempt to steal their eggs. As they move upstream, both male and female alter drastically, especially the males. The hens turn a gray, rusty brown, and the cocks transform from thick, smooth, polished torpedoes to humpbacked creatures with distorted-looking hooked jaws and long teeth as their colors alter to bright red to rusty red then to gray black. By the end of their monumental spawning run, they "Jekyll and Hyde" into thin, dark, gaunt, scarred, fungus-covered ghosts of their sea-run physical perfection and eventually die, their massive frames greatly contributing to the chain of life for both land and water creatures.

My first encounters catching these royal fish were in Michigan on the Boyne River. Casting upstream and drifting steelhead/coho flies by

The sight of an unexpected fifty-pound, male king salmon tail walking at the end of your line and realizing that it's connected to your favorite trout or steelhead rod burns a memory that you'll always be able to vividly recall.

groups of kings, I hooked several that repeatedly jumped, tail walked, and charged downstream, and I just couldn't stop them—in fact, they seemed to get stronger the longer they were on the fly! I assume this is because they must have the ability to generate so much power to successfully cope with all the obstacles in their historically long migration routes. Over the decades, on light tackle, I've unintentionally had kings take my fly while steelhead and rainbow fishing in British Columbia and Alaska. I eventually learned, when I hooked a king, to just point my rod at it, dig in my wader heels, and break the tippet. Kings are so brutally strong and long-winded that you need to be equipped with powerful fly tackle and be ready to use brute strength to compete with them. Because kings are so physically large, it's common to foul hook them. When this happens, just go ahead and break off the fly to cut the loss of time, strength, and purpose for both you and the king.

Author/editor Tom Pero once told me that he thought that fresh-from-the-ocean Chinooks of the Dean River tidal pools were the strongest fish that swim in fresh water—and were his favorites. Rods of 10- to 12-weight, 20-pound tippets, strong arms, and a broad back are standard for those who want to consistently hook, battle, and land these beauties. Witnessing an unexpected, massive four-foot crimson-silver missile launch into a series of downstream, arm-wrenching tail walks will burn deep and thrilling memories for life!

Giant Chinook salmon, especially truly wild ones, are such a valuable gift of nature. Because of dams, clear-cut timbering, spawning bed deterioration, pollution, overfishing, and interbreeding with inferior hatchery fish, wild Chinooks are becoming more rare in North America and especially in California, Oregon, and Washington, perhaps down to 10 percent of their former, untampered-with-by-man numbers. At this time excellent angling for wild kings still exists along the coast, tidal pools, and first miles up major rivers in British Columbia and Alaska. With increased understanding and help from all who use the resources, we hope that wild Chinooks will always be king of the Pacific Salmon.

CHAPTER 20

COHO SALMON
(Oncorhynchus kisutch)

Coho, or silver, are very special Pacific salmon because of their aggressiveness for striking flies and lures while at sea as well as during their spawning runs up West Coast rivers from northern California to Alaska and the Great Lakes. These salmon average six to ten pounds, which also happens to be the ideal size to create fast, strong runs and impressive and numerous water-clearing vaults on light fly and spin tackle. In the Pacific Ocean, they mostly range close to shore along the continental shelf, feeding on diverse food forms, such as herring, shell fish, crustaceans, and squid. Here they also readily rise to streamer flies, spoons, and lures that suggest these foods.

Dave Whitlock

Coho salmon, once they enter freshwater to spawn, cannot eat, but they will eagerly rise and strike colorful flies—even at the surface. It's always interesting to see what color phase each hookup brings. The fresher, more silver females leap highest and fight hardest, but the brilliantly colored, large-kyped males are so fascinating to look at and photograph.

Coho enter streams to spawn exactly where they were spawned, if possible, in September and October, after one to two years of living in the open ocean or the Great Lakes. On this upstream movement, they stop to rest in pools and backwaters and/or tributary inlets, where they have little hesitation about rising repeatedly to brightly colored, swinging flies, even on the surface, or to spoons and spinning lures.

Once hooked, they steak away in fast, long, downstream runs and frequent water-clearing leaps. My first encounter with silvers was in September on Bristol Bay's Togiak River and is still vivid in my memory. I hooked nine the first morning and managed to land only one! I just couldn't keep up with their long, streaking downstream runs. Those Alaskan silvers were about six- to ten-pounders but in the Great Lakes, where silvers were introduced in 1966, they easily exceed these average weights, often reaching ten to twelve pounds or more in years when alewife and smelt population peak. The current world record of thirty-three pounds four ounces is a Great Lakes fish, coming from a tributary of the Salmon River of Lake Ontario in 1989.

Silvers are elegantly chrome plated while they are at sea, but once on their spawning runs in September and October, they become more fantastically colorful each day. As they move upstream, the colors on their silver sides begin to tarnish with golden hues, pinks, reddish-orange, or copper and rusty red. I'm always fascinated by the wide variety of color phases in any big school of migrating cohos. The males grow an almost comical, over-sized kype (upper and lower jaw) that for me resembles the droopy nose of an elephant seal.

Most silvers have spawning runs of less than 100 miles upstream. Often, however, wild silvers in the Columbia and Yukon Rivers must travel 500 to 1,400 miles to their ancestral spawning gravels. Like all Pacific salmon, silvers die shortly after spawning. Eggs hatch by spring, and the coho parr emerge from their incubating gravel and spend about one year in freshwater rivers, where they grow four to six inches long. At that point, as if given some invisible signal, they become chrome-colored smolts and swim down river and out to the ocean, where they will stay and grow for sixteen to eighteen months and then start the long trek back up their birth rivers to begin their one and only spawn. A small percentage of males will live in the ocean for only one year before moving back into the rivers to attempt to spawn. This unorthodox early male maturation is another great example of how nature attempts to ensure species survival and healthy, genetic diversity.

Coho are a perfect match for 7- and 8-weight fly tackle. The most popular fly line is the No. 4 or 5 sinking tip, which is ideal to swing coho streamers in four to twelve feet of water just above the concentrations of fish that rest near the bottoms of pools and backwaters. A floating line is required if you'd like to lure them to the surface to attack waking hair and foam flies, an opportunity no coho flyfisher should miss out on. It seems silver salmon are most excited during their spawning runs by flies that are from 6 to 1/0 in size and in the brightest colors of pink, orange, and metallic silver, purple, and blue. I've often thought that they seem most attracted to the same colors that magically appear on their extraordinary forms.

Silver salmon populations have been heavily impacted by man's environmental and overfishing exploitations in California, Oregon, and Washington. Wild varieties still existing in the states are further endangered by farmed salmon and the diseases and genetic dilution that they

Coho salmon are most attracted to surface and subsurface flies that are garnished brightly with pink, orange, purple, and silver.

bring to the game. Today the best wild silver fishing in North America is throughout British Columbia and Alaska. Some Chilean rivers provide silver fishing from escapees of salmon farming during their spawning efforts.

Fresh-from-the-ocean silver salmon remind me so much of steelhead in size, shape, leaping, and fighting ability, but fortunately they are generally easier to raise on flies than steelhead. They are truly a special gift to flyfishers and to the eyes of the beholder. They are the second-least-abundant Pacific salmon, but it's hard to believe that when you are swinging your flies over a magnificent, big, fresh run.

CHAPTER 21

SOCKEYE SALMON
(*Oncorhynchus nerka*)

One of the most dramatic sights I've witnessed is an Alaska or British Columbia river packed with radiant, crimson and golden-olive, spawning sockeye salmon. Sockeyes are magnificent, and their abundance, beauty, and willingness to take flies and lures, as well as their almost fluorescent-red flesh and absolutely delicious flavor, make sockeye a highly prized catch.

Sockeye are sometimes called big red salmon or blue backs and are next to the smallest of the Pacific salmon, averaging twenty-two to twenty-six inches and seven pounds. But in commercial value and brilliant color, they have no equal.

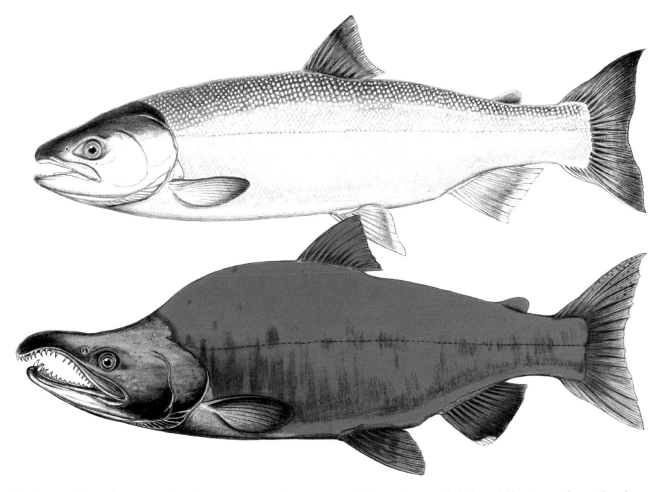

Sockeye adults, when returning from the ocean to spawn, quickly undergo a Jekyll-and-Hyde transformation from torpedo-like, blue-backed, chrome-plated bodies to a grotesque, tooth-filled snout and a humpbacked, crimson-bodied salmon in just a few upstream swimming days.

In western North America, they are most abundant from the Fraser River of British Columbia to Bristol Bay, Alaska, but can be caught as far south as the Columbia River and north to the Yukon River. The most successful populations exist where there are no dams and where large, natural lakes connect to rivers that outlet into the Pacific Ocean. This is because sockeye parr must have still waters or at least backwaters of rivers in order to feed on the zooplankton and invertebrates associated with still waters—the most important being the one-sixteenth-inch-long Daphnia crustacean commonly known as the water flea.

Sockeye are early fall spawners that, depending on their family group, spawn either in two to three weeks or two to three months after beginning their freshwater runs up rivers. They can spawn in rivers or small streams, at the mouths of small lake inlets, along the shorelines of lakes, and even in moderate-depth lake gravels. They all die shortly after spawning, completing their next important contribution—their bodies become food and fertilizer for the entire ecosystem within their home-water range.

Hatching in early spring, the one-and-a-half-inch sockeye fry emerge from the gravel redds by late spring and feed on zooplankton, crustaceans, aquatic insect nymphs, and larvae. When they reach three to six inches, they begin to smolt, changing to a brilliant silver color. This may happen within one year or take up to three years.

In the spring, sockeye smolt swim downstream to the Pacific Ocean and spend the next four to six years feeding heavily on ocean crustaceans, fish, and squid. During these years at sea, sockeye grow to their full size of twenty-two to twenty-six inches and four to seven pounds. Some regions produce adults up to thirty-three inches and fifteen pounds.

When sockeye mature, like all Pacific salmon, they return to their home rivers as radiantly silver beauties with iridescent blue backs and robust, firm bodies. In the first tidal pools, they are quick to strike small, brightly colored flies, spoons, jigs, and spinners, and they provide a spectacular battle on light-line tackle. As the schools swim upstream toward their very specific destinations, they quickly undergo drastic body and color changes. The males develop a long-jawed kype and fierce, long teeth. Large, high humps develop on their backs and their chrome-colored scale coats change to a breathtaking scarlet-red over most of their body while their heads become a deep, golden olive accented with black. When colors are at their peak, thickly grouped schools of crimson and green sockeye can actually change the glow of the water. These schools can easily be seen from the air by lodge float planes and are sure indicators of good fishing for the char and rainbows that follow them in search of their eggs.

Sockeye females dig gravel redds into which one or more females deposit their 3,000 to 6,000 deep red-orange eggs. Within a few days, the spawned-out, spent salmon bodies quickly deteriorate and soon die. Their bodies are either eaten by other trout, eagles, bears, gulls, ravens, and others or disintegrate into nutrients on the bottoms of the stream or in piles along the shoreline. Strangely, there is little putrid decomposition odor connected with the scene.

Sockeye are excellent, hard-fighting, light-tackle game fish that take small, brightly colored artificials readily as they begin their runs to spawn. However, by the time they reach the spawning grounds, most have lost their vigor and interest in taking flies and lures. Males commonly fight one another or the trout and char that are attempting to grab their eggs. I've had males bite my swim fins as I swam among them

Thickly grouped schools of crimson and golden-green sockeye can dramatically change the glow of a river.

taking underwater photos. At this time, egg and sculpin flies fished around the redds may take some males but will mostly result in nice catches of egg-stealing rainbow, Arctic char, and Dolly Varden. I believe these salmon are mostly hooked by accident as flies are breathed in or caught on their skin or fins before the fly can drift into the reaches of a trout or char.

My most long-lasting and truly surrealistic sockeye experience was at Bristol Bay in Alaska at a small inlet tributary to a lovely, large lake. The turquoise-colored inlet was absolutely packed with

red salmon, eagles were soaring overhead, and it was showering. Just as I hooked a big, tail-walking male sockeye, the sun broke through the clouds and created a big, magnificent rainbow in the sky. I still remember it as if it were yesterday.

Wild sockeye salmon populations in the areas that I've mentioned are reasonably secure because conservation groups such as TU are keeping a close watch on the 100-million-pound annual commercial harvest, and on mining, land development, and dam construction. I hope every reader and his or her children will have the breathtaking experience of witnessing a spawning run of sockeye and feeling their wild spirits against the arch of your fly rod.

Kokanee Salmon

Sockeye salmon have a miniature lake form, the Kokanee, or little red salmon, that never run to the sea. Historically, both forms occurred in numerous watersheds, but over the ages some sockeye lake outlets have been blocked from the sea, and there, only Kokanee survive.

Kokanee closely resemble their sea-run counterparts in shape, coloration, and life cycle but are much smaller, ranging from seven to twenty inches as adults. They have been stocked successfully in numerous western lakes and are popular with trolling trout anglers and flyfishers when they congregate to spawn at lake inlets.

CHAPTER 22

CHUM SALMON
(Oncorhynchus keta)

Chum salmon, also known as calico or dog salmon, are the second-largest Pacific salmon in size and make up what some estimate to be the largest Pacific salmon species biomass when the wild and commercially ranched populations are combined. Chum are common on short West Coast rivers, from central Oregon to western Alaska, and there are even some runs in the Arctic Ocean's Mackenzie River drainage. Likewise, there are populations in Asia as far south as Korea, but they are most abundant as wild runs in Russia and hatchery runs in Japan.

As they enter and run up their home rivers to spawn, they are aggressive at striking flies and lures but not especially popular with sport anglers because they don't make spectacular jumps and their flesh has inferior texture, color, and taste compared to the red-fleshed kings, coho, and sockeye salmon. This is mainly due to the low fat content of their bodies. However, they can offer the flyfisher a real battle. Most chum that I've caught were those that took my flies while I was fishing for steelhead. They gave me a long, dogged fight that terminated in a neat visual surprise of their striking shape and unique colorations—and, of course, mandatory photos.

The body of a mature male chum is as robust in shape, width, and thickness as, or even more than, any other Pacific salmon species. It is built for swift swimming, being very streamlined with a sharply pointed nose and strong, sloping shoulders tapering quickly to an extra-large, rigid tail.

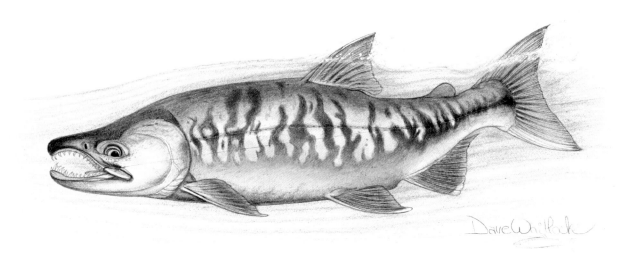

The chum salmon is also called calico salmon. One look at this beautifully colored and marked prime spawning male makes the reason obvious. Landing one of these strong males creates a mandatory photographic opportunity.

Even the dorsal fin is positioned farther back to provide additional speed. The chum is perfectly designed for clearing waterfalls, making fast-river ascents, and bending fly rods. What captivates me most is the spotless, light golden-olive tinting, fading to paler silvery-olive background below the lateral line, again shading to dark olive, pink, maroon, and black near its underside. Then, as

Hormone-charged chum salmon, approaching short coastal rivers from the Pacific, rapidly change from sea-bright silver coloration to an intricate calico pattern of many colors. Undergoing drastic head and body shape changes, they quickly jump waterfalls and shoot up rapids and riffles to find their spawning gravels in a short, fast race with time before they perish.

if an artist turned him on his back and let those paints run with gravity, the colors form intriguing multicolor or calico tiger-like vertical stripes.

From their simple ocean colors of blue or turquoise backs and mirror-bright silver sides, this most intricate Pacific salmon coloration quickly blooms when they reach their home river intertidal zones and they take the first day's taste of freshwater. It's easy to understand, looking at such a fish, why some call them calico salmon. The dog salmon name is a bit less obvious. Explanations run from their big set of dog teeth to its reference by a native fishermen who reserved the chum, with its inferior taste and texture, for drying into dog meat. Most chum salmon used for human consumption is marketed as silverbrite salmon and is usually canned.

Chum salmon live an average of three to five years. Their life cycle begins with spawning in the southern range from September through December and earlier in the north. When fry emerge, they feed on aquatic invertebrates as they swim down to the sea in their first year of life, with very little time spent feeding in streams. The fry tend to feed in estuaries and then move northward along the coast before migrating to the open ocean, where they will feed until they mature and return to spawn. In their intertidal and ocean habitats, they aggressively feed and quickly develop on a diet of zooplankton, fish, shrimp, and squid. However, adult chum salmon are distinguished by a diet that is much more heavily dominated by jellyfish and other soft-bodied prey, compared to other Pacific salmon species.

Most chum spawning populations are found in shorter coastal rivers, which they seek out. They usually spawn not long after entering the mouths of the rivers before they rapidly deteriorate and die. However, a few chum do run up large rivers such as the Yukon and Mackenzie and are on record as swimming upriver an amazing 1,700 miles. I'm always fascinated how species evolve to fit every niche of their environment and coexist within that environment with other native species. I wish we were more like that.

The current angler world-record chum is a whopping thirty-five pounds and was caught in British Columbia in 1995. Undocumented weights up to forty-six pounds have been reported. Such extreme departures from their average weight, which is nine to ten pounds, are the result of an extra year or two at sea, allowing them to feed up, and often the lack of sexual development. These largest specimens are always male. Bright steelhead flies or those that work well for sockeye and kings will take chums consistently. Seven- and 8-weight rods with sink-tip or full-sinking lines are best to swing flies over the bottom-hugging positions of chums in runs and pools. Because spawning fish decline so quickly, the closer to tidewater the better for the best-conditioned, aggressive, fresh-from-the-sea chums on fly tackle and on the dinner table.

Typical of all North American salmon, chum have been impacted by human development on their home streams, and, in fact, several such areas are listed as having endangered populations and are fully protected. Although not the most popular salmon to fish for or eat, chum are fine fish and serve many important uses in nature and for man as they carry out their amazing life cycle.

CHAPTER 23

PINK SALMON
(*Oncorhynchus gorbuscha*)

Pink salmon, also known as humpback salmon, are truly an amazing paradox, being the smallest salmon of North American Pacific salmon, averaging three and a half to five pounds, having the shortest life span, yet making up the largest wild-living biomass of all salmon. They develop from eggs to egg-depositing adults in only *two* years. This relatively short life cycle is possible because after the fry hatch, instead of living in streams before migrating to sea, they go directly downstream and are ready to live in salt water the day they emerge from the redds. At sea they spend fourteen to eighteen months in offshore waters, feeding on fish, squid, and crus-

The pink salmon at sea resembles the other four Pacific salmon species in general shape and color, but within a few days of entering freshwater to spawn, the males undergo a rapid shape and coloration transformation.

taceans before they mature and return to their home rivers, usually during July, August, and September. Pinks spawn in rivers that are typically not more than thirty to forty miles long or only travel short distances up longer rivers to spawn and then perish into the life-giving food chain. Because they are all two years old when they spawn, pink salmon of one generation do not spawn with the generation before or after them, a unique trait among salmon that is described as creating "even-odd year classes." This means that 2013-born fish would not have the opportunity to spawn with 2012- or 2014-born pinks.

The Pacific range for North American pinks is from the streams of Puget Sound in Washington to near Canada's Mackenzie River (but they are rare in the Arctic Ocean) and several of the Aleutian Islands. They were accidently introduced into Lake Superior in 1956, where they survive, but because of the lake's very cold temperature and low fertility, they average a meager one to two pounds. However, due to their innate nature to stray from their home rivers, they have eventually populated all of the Great Lakes. Even more bizarre, a huge specimen (thirteen pounds one ounce) was caught in the Great Lakes in 1992. Pinks were also introduced into Atlantic Ocean drainages and thrived for short periods, but no significant populations exist there today.

Although pink salmon are small, they are a fascinating sight, being such miniatures, and are a real treat for photographers, both above and below the water. They have the typical dark metallic backs and chrome-like side colors of other Pacific salmon when they are at sea but rapidly transform into a vivid color scheme of blues and turquoises on their upper head, back, and dorsal fin, blending to rich accents of red, rust, and oranges on their gill plates, along their mid to posterior lateral line and entire tail. Their

sides and stomach, below the lateral line, turn to a pearly ivory white, and all the lower fins become brightly colored with white, orange, and shades of indigo blues. On the tops of their backs to their lateral line, adipose fin, and tail, large, vivid and distinctive blackish spots develop—real little beauties in my opinion. The males grow long, graceful kypes and impressive rows of kype and jaw teeth. But it is their high, arching, humped backs in front of the dorsal fin that is most eye-catching and, of course, the reason for their "humpy" nickname. Females are similarly colored and marked but do not develop the hump.

Pink salmon will strike steelhead flies and typical salmon attractor flies, lures, spoons, and spinners—trolled at sea or drifted in rivers—just in smaller sizes. When targeting pinks, using trout-caliber rods of 4, 5, and 6 weights or light spin tackle makes them much more fun to engage. Like chum salmon, their closest evolutionary relatives, pinks are at their strongest and best condition when hooked in estuaries or just a few miles above tidewater. They deteriorate very rapidly once they reach their spawning areas.

Because they spend a large proportion of their life cycle ocean-feeding and usually spawn short distances up their rivers, pink salmon are not as dependent on freshwater as other salmon and so are less vulnerable to human impact on their habitats; thus, they are not as endangered in their natural North American and Great Lakes ranges. Because of their smaller sizes and less desirable white-to-pink flesh—similar to chum salmon—pinks are not as well known or popular to anglers of Pacific species. Most are commercially harvested and end up as canned salmon.

Writing and illustrating this profile series about the five Pacific salmon has given me a much better perspective of the life of these magnificent fish. I truly hope it has done the same for you.

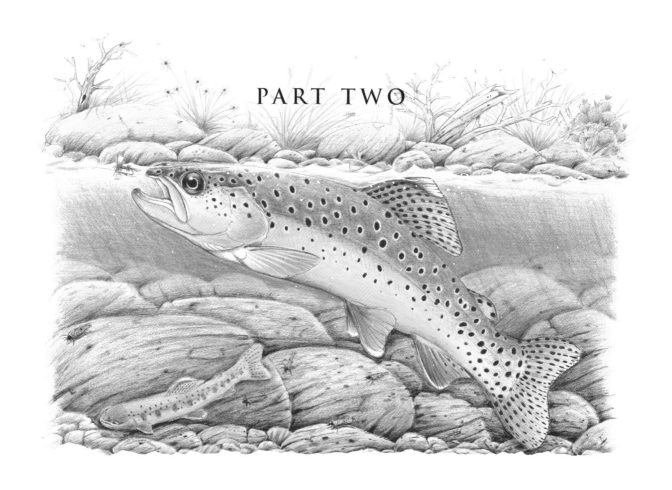

PART TWO

THE FLIES THAT CATCH THEM

CHAPTER 24

TROUT FLIES

Trout flies have always been a fascinating mix of practical function, unique sculptural form, and hypnotic beauty to me. In the next few chapters, I'd like to discuss wet flies, dry flies, nymphs, emergers, crustaceans, terrestrials, streamers, bottom dwellers, and exciters/ attractors, and how I see their evolution, from historic, to traditional standards, to new designs. The materials, performances, and effectiveness will receive my analysis, as will their colors and forms through my pens, pencils, and paints.

As you know, most trout flies are imitations of some form of live trout food. I believe the term *fly* evolved from a general British description of insects, much like Americans use the word *bugs*. Originally, most trout flies were imitations of *aquatic* insects, both mature and immature. However, as the sport of fly fishing spread and evolved to many places in the world, and as more fly fishing was done throughout the entire four seasons, flyfishers recognized that trout indeed feed on much more than just aquatic insects. Paralleling this, flyfish-

ers slowly accepted that it was good sport to fish flies not only on the surface, but throughout the entire water column of streams and lakes.

During my lifetime, in order to reach deeper depths and fish swifter waters, many American trout flies have been gradually tied with heavier

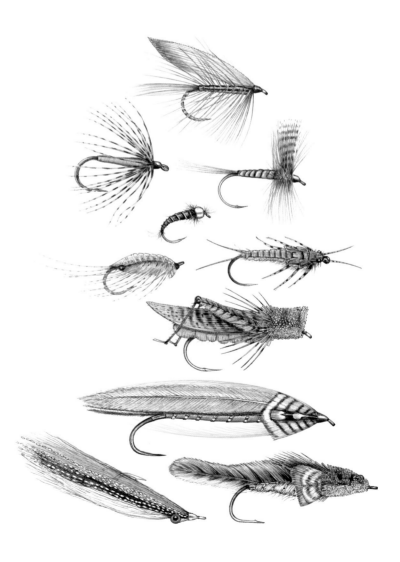

Trout feed on an awesome variety of food forms and so a typical fly selection should include wet flies, soft hackles, dry flies, midges, crustaceans, nymphs, terrestrials, streamers, lead-eyed streamers, bottom minnows.

and heavier materials, for example, copper wire, bead chain eyes, lead wire, lead eyes, and very dense tungsten beads are employed (as well as using split-shot and fast-sinking fly line) to get these flies down deep. As this "weight race" began, many older flyfishers on both continents strongly objected. I remember that Lee Wulff, perhaps our most acclaimed wild trout conservationist, argued that trout and salmon need water depth for sanctuary to survive our fishing efforts. Weighted flies and fly lines have taken much of that away from them. There are still a few trout and salmon waters (mostly in Europe, but also in America) where weighted flies and lines are forbidden.

So, the simple definition of a fly has changed greatly over time and has gotten much more complex.

When I was eight years old, I didn't realize it but I began making fly-like lures when I'd run out of worms, bacon fat, crawfish tails, or whatever bait I was able to find for catching bluegill and bullheads on my cane pole. I'd tie bits of grass, feathers, rubber bands, and other odds and ends to my long-shank cricket hooks, using red sewing thread I'd get from my grandmother. By gosh, these crudest of imitations worked pretty well! I've been designing and tying flies ever since, without any lull in my enthusiasm.

Through my teens and early twenties, I continued to create flies that worked for me with what limited tools, materials, and instructions I could find in the 1940s and 1950s in Oklahoma. This self-educating process proved to be a minor handicap—and a major advantage—during my lifetime as a creative trout fly designer and tier.

One of my first impressions about trout fly tying, after learning about many of the famous trout flies, was that they had to be constructed of only very specific natural animal feathers and hair, such as otter, jungle cock, and wood duck. I considered these materials to be almost sacred and magical in their ability to imitate live trout foods. Yet my "home-made," unorthodox flies, spun with the hair from local rabbits and squirrels I hunted and barnyard rooster feathers, would also catch trout—at least in the stocked streams in Missouri state parks and in the Smoky Mountain streams I personally could reach from Oklahoma.

As I matured into my early thirties, I realized a couple of important facts. One, many of these "famous trout flies" had been constructed by early tiers using, like I had, materials that were available to them locally. Second, I could use synthetic materials that would be similar in color, texture, and physical dimensions to the natural materials. Synthetics signaled a departure

Flies not usually considered standard trout food imitations: eggs, worms, pellets, microjigs.

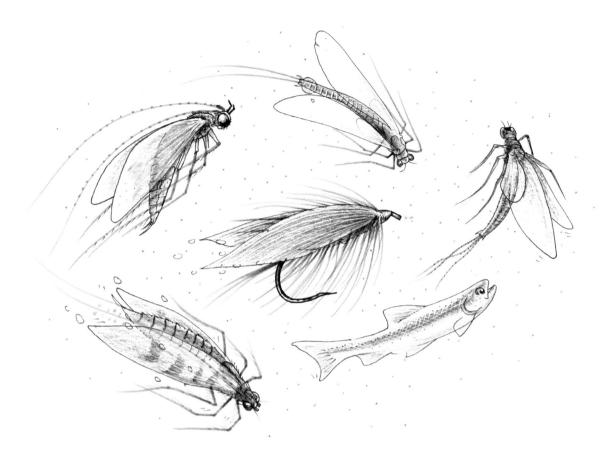

A trout fly can simulate several food forms. The ones that suggest the widest variety of foods often become standards or classics.

from traditional materials, and that took some time to be accepted by the majority of older tiers and flyfishers. But these materials became more and more important as the supplies of natural, wild materials around the world dwindled and/ or they became unlawful or unethical to collect or sell. Today, most naturals are raised or legally hunted specifically for the garment industry or fishing-lure market.

Although I still love to tie with natural materials the most, I have extended my fly designing significantly with synthetic hair, furs, foams, silicone, latex, Mylars, wires, paints, molding compounds, nylon threads, and plastic eyes. I would not want to go back to those limiting days of using only natural materials. I want my designs first to cater to trout, but at the same time, to

be attractive to flyfishers as useful and durable artistic sculptures of trout foods.

Today, I don't envy fly buyers at the dealer or retailer level. There are so many choices of all types of trout flies. How does one choose the best flies? I hope my series will help you to better choose an effective fly to buy or tie for your fly-fishing situation, even if it is an "old standard," and not always just what's new and different. Trout foods don't change every year, so it's not absolutely necessary to reinvent their imitation, although it can be fun to do so. My goal for this new series is to help flyfishers to more fully understand and value trout flies as functional art forms—whether they have been created over the last four centuries or created at home with your own efforts.

Let's see where this takes us!

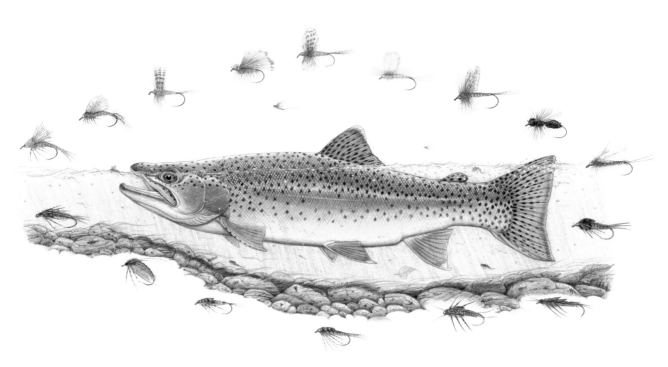

The hallmark of fly fishing for trout is to try to match the natural foods on which they are feeding. I call this piece "Hatches and Matches."

CHAPTER 25

THE TRADITIONAL WET FLY

Nearly five centuries ago, trout anglers began fly fishing with traditional wet flies. These first flies were conceived to imitate various forms of natural insects and colorful attractor forms with the hope of triggering strikes. Wet flies are still used today and are constructed on small, heavy-wire hooks to ensure sinking and tied precisely with sparse amounts of soft, water-absorbing feathers, hairs, and metallic tinsel to create swimming forms and patterns that catch a trout's eye and trigger their aggressive feeding responses. Today, flyfishers recognize the term *wet fly* a bit differently as simply descriptive of flies that sink below the water's surface, such as nymphs, soft hackles, and steelhead and Atlantic salmon flies and streamers.

Traditional wet flies have a specific shape and appearance that sets them apart from other "sinking-flies." Their form is simplistic, captivating, and unique. Once you've seen them, you will easily recognize them. When I was a child, the first trout flies I remember seeing were traditional-type, gut-snelled

wet flies. I especially loved the ones with quill-segment paired wings. I now see them as some of the purest sculptures of fishing lures, so beautiful, yet so entirely functional. It may come as a surprise that these classic "old" flies are still some of the most effective trout flies you can use today to fish our North American streams and still waters. Until I was properly introduced into the art of tying and fishing these traditionals, I also thought them to be only antiques of the past and mainly for the "less skilled" among us.

Years ago, while shopping at Dan Bailey's store in Livingston, Montana, I saw an eight-pound brown a man brought in to register for the "Wall of Fame." He said he had caught it on a size 10, *Cow Dung* wet fly. I simply refused to believe he was telling the truth. Today, I have no doubt that indeed he had caught it on that classic wet fly.

These days, my most favorite method for catching trout is the traditional wet-fly fishing way, using two or three flies where allowed. These flies and the technique to use them are utterly mesmerizing and allow the flyfisher to

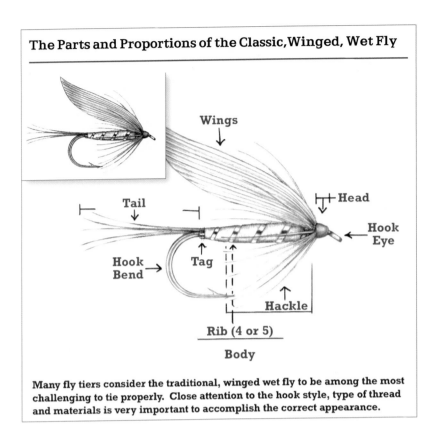

The Parts and Proportions of the Classic, Winged, Wet Fly

Wings

Tail

Head

Hook Eye

Hook Bend

Tag

Hackle

Rib (4 or 5)

Body

Many fly tiers consider the traditional, winged wet fly to be among the most challenging to tie properly. Close attention to the hook style, type of thread and materials is very important to accomplish the correct appearance.

be very proactive. I love the aggression that trout display, especially larger, wild browns, as I animate the flies. Each time I tie, fish, or talk about traditional wet flies, I think how fortunate I am that over two decades ago Davy Wotton moved from Wales to northeastern Arkansas and taught me the traditional methods handed down through the centuries. I've been one of his disciples ever since!

Another surprise about traditional wet flies is that Davy, and many other noted trout fly tiers, consider tying wet flies correctly to be more challenging than tying most nymphs, emergers, dry flies, or streamers. Precisely selecting the correct textures and colors of the natural feathers, hair, tinsel, and silk floss, and then tying them in the exact shape, proportion, and position so they are balanced and swim correctly take very skillful attention. This challenge, however, is extremely gratifying. I was surprised at how poorly I did on

my first attempts to tie and illustrate these flies. Now that I've learned much more, illustrating this feature was a dream—and I can even tie them adequately.

Traditional winged wet flies are usually unweighted, size 10, 12, and 14, and fished two or three on a leader attached to a floating double-taper line. The rods are usually size 4, 5, or 6, midflex taper, and 9, 10, and 11 feet long. This arrangement provides ideal fly presentation, mending, and animation. If three flies are used, two natural patterns and one attractor is the most popular choice. An imitator and attractor combo is ideal with two flies. The wet-fly method philosophy, as I see it, is to attract and trigger a trout's natural feeding response to insect forms that move as though they were alive, yet totally vulnerable to catch. In my experience, most trout, especially brown trout, take traditional wets with a fast, strong rush and then an instant

Ten realistic traditional winged wet flies. These patterns suggest realistic insects, although the Wickman's Fancy and McGinty are also used as attractors. Top to bottom: Wickman's Fancy, Iron Blue Dun, Lead Wing Coachman, McGinty, Gold Ribbed Hare's Ear, Ginger Quill, Greenwell's Glory, March Brown, Cow Dung, Invicta.

Ten attractor traditional winged wet flies (top to bottom): Silver Doctor, Alexandra, Brook Fin, Scarlet Ibis, Orange Sedge, Yellow Sally, Royal Coachman, Montreal, Bloody Butcher, Parmachene Belle.

Note: These twenty flies have all proven reputations for catching trout consistently over the last four hundred years.

change of direction, which results in self-hooking and lots of break offs, especially if your tippet is weak or your strike response is just a bit aggressive. I seldom use lighter than 3X tippet to cope with these spine-tingling takes! Since most traditional wet-fly fishing is done by presenting and animating the flies across and downstream, the angle encourages a trout to dash downstream, easily doubling their fighting advantage against your tackle.

Beautiful and graceful, classic traditional winged wet flies may be among the oldest fly designs, but they are also extremely timely and effective for both experienced and new flyfishers to lure trout. I'll wager that most trout, wild or hatchery-raised, that are swimming in North American waters have yet to see their first tra-

ditional wet flies seductively presented to their dining areas. For many of you readers, these flies can easily be the newest and most exciting way to experience this nearly five-century-old sport. I predict that in the next two or three years, traditional wet-fly fishing will become the hottest trend in fly fishing.

Note: I recommend Davy Wotton's DVD *Wet Fly Ways*, as well as Edson Leonard's book *Flies* (AS Barnes & Co, 1960), Ray Bergman's *Trout* (Alfred Knopf, 1962), and Mike Valla's *The Classic Wet Fly Box*, (Whitefish Press, 2012). There are very few classic winged traditional wet flies available in fly shops at this time, so we are carrying Davy Wotton's flies and DVD on our website: www .davewhitlock.com

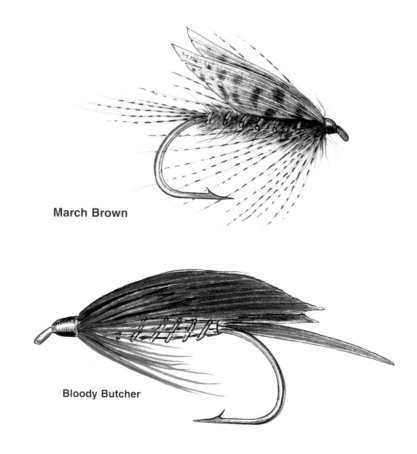

March Brown

Bloody Butcher

CHAPTER 26

THE TRADITIONAL DRY FLY

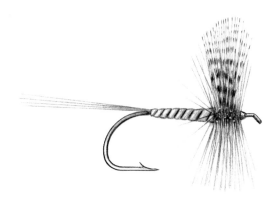

Since its conception in the 1800s, the dry fly has been an important mainstay in most every trout fisher's fly box. It may be that beautiful, aquatic mayfly adults—most likely *Ephemera danica*—floating like delicate sailboats on the smooth surface of English chalk streams inspired man to first fly fish for trout. The design, effectiveness, grace, beauty, and charm of these flies have captured the devotion of fly-fishing writers, poets, artists, and fly tiers throughout the centuries. I was so moved when I first witnessed this *danica* emergence on the Itchen in Hampshire, England. The experience of seeing a trout rise to the surface and capture a mayfly, and then rise again to an imitation of the mayfly you've just presented, is a moving experience that is seldom forgotten and addictive to the degree that some trout flyfishers never fish any other way again.

Just as the basic definition of a wet fly is a fly that sinks into the water, the dry fly is a fly that floats on water. Actually, most dry flies are captured in the water surface film, leaving some or most of the fly extended above the surface. My references suggest that the traditional dry fly was originally created to imitate duns and spinners of *Ephemera*—the mayfly—by Frederick Halford, who lived in England in the late 1800s. After the traditional dry fly was well established in Europe, Theodore Gordon, an American enamored with Halford's work, began tying and then fishing these flies in the Catskills and other northeastern trout waters around 1889. American fly-fishing historians affectionately honor Mr. Gordon with the esteemed title of "Father of the American Dry Fly," and his Quill Gordon is most symbolic of the traditional dry fly in North America.

These early dry flies, on both continents, were considered practical only on calm, slow-moving chalk streams, spring creeks, and still waters. But after Emlyn Gill wrote *Practical Dry-Fly Fishing* in 1912, followed by George LaBranche's *The Dry Fly and Fast Water* in 1914, the fly's acceptance on our faster-flowing trout streams began and has continued in popularity and design development ever since.

Here in the United States, traditional dry flies are often known as "Catskill" dry flies. Delicate

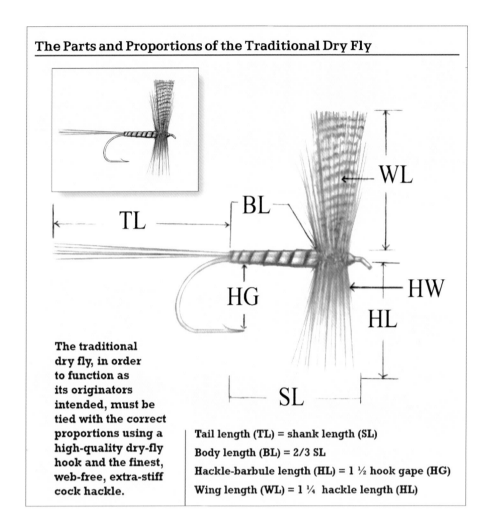

The Parts and Proportions of the Traditional Dry Fly

WL

BL

TL

HG

HW

HL

SL

The traditional dry fly, in order to function as its originators intended, must be tied with the correct proportions using a high-quality dry-fly hook and the finest, web-free, extra-stiff cock hackle.

Tail length (TL) = shank length (SL)

Body length (BL) = 2/3 SL

Hackle-barbule length (HL) = 1 ½ hook gape (HG)

Wing length (WL) = 1 ¼ hackle length (HL)

and beautiful, they are designed and constructed to alight softly on the surface film and to rest upright and mostly above the surface, as does the mayfly dun that it most frequently imitates. To achieve this performance, it is tied on a small, very-light wire hook with extra-fine silk or nylon thread, using the finest-sized cock hackle, duck-wing feather segments, duck breast or flank

From left to right: mayfly dun sits on top of the surface film with only leg tips protruding below the surface; the hypothetical perfect float for a traditional dry fly; the more typical float of a traditional dry fly attached to the leader. Note how the hook and part of the barbules protrude below the surface.

Twelve traditional Catskill-style dry flies, with the mayfly dun most are meant to imitate. These beautiful Catskill imitations are examples of the wonderful tying skills of Rube Cross, Winnie and Walt Dette, Harry and Elise Darbee, and Art Flick.

Flies, top to bottom and right to left—Gray Fox Variant, Red Quill, Whirling Blue Dun, Light Cahill, Greenwell's Glory, Hendrickson, March Brown, Ginger Quill, Quill Gordon, Pale Evening Dun, Adams, Dun Variant.

feathers, herl, hackle stems, and water-animal fur. To create perfect balance, the wings, hackle, thorax, body, tails, and heads call for very stringent proportions, and little or no cement is used. The most important imitative characteristics of the traditional dry fly are the wings, then thorax, abdomen, legs, and lastly the tail. This priority was established from observation of what was thought a trout sees from its underwater eye view of mayfly duns and spinners on the surface as they float into the window of the trout's vision. The order of importance for choosing and fishing the fly was then thought to be: size, presentation, color, form, buoyancy, and transparency.

The hypothetical *perfect* float position of the traditional dry fly is seldom, if ever, achieved because of the fly's connection to the line and leader, the way it is tied, the presentation, the condition of the water surface, and how well it actually floats. The hook and hackle barbules often protrude well below the surface in an unnatural manner. Yet trout, wild and tame, eagerly take this less-than-perfect imitation if presented with an acceptable size, color, and good drift. Discussions among flyfishers and tiers on why this is so are wonderfully thought-provoking. My own observation is that trout display a different rise action to the traditional dry fly than they do to the naturals, which seems to imply that, in the trout's opinion, the variations are acceptable within their opportunistic feeding drive and limited reasoning.

The traditional dry fly patterns mostly reflect the general color and marking patterns of the mayfly hatches indigenous to the waters being fished, or as Ernest Schwiebert coined it, "matching the hatch," in his book of the same title in 1955. These patterns are mostly duns (gray), sulfurs (pale yellows), and olives. The attractor traditional dry flies, such as the Royal Coachman, were seldom as popular among the Catskill dry-fly purists.

If you'd like to know more about traditional dry flies and how to tie the classic patterns, I'd recommend the following:

Ray Bergman's *Trout*, (Alfred Knopf, 1962).
J. Edson Leonard's *Flies* (A.S. Barnes & Co., 1960).
Darrel Martin's *The Fly-Fisher's Craft* (Skyhorse Publishing, 2016).
Art Flick's *Streamside Guide* (Crown Publishers, 1969).
Ernest Schwiebert's *Matching the Hatch* (Macmillan Co., 1955).

Each of these provides a special historic viewpoint of the traditional dry fly.

The traditional dry fly is still popular today, especially in our eastern streams and still waters. The good news for this design is that we are constantly improving on the hooks, threads, and tying materials, especially the extra-high-quality genetic cock hackle. The high-floating fly lines, tapered leader designs, and wonderful rods available today also enable us to be more successful at casting, presenting, drifting, and catching with these delicate flies. There are usually assortments of traditional dry flies available in fly shops and website stores. However, there truly is a magic to finding just the right materials and fine hooks and correctly tying to proportion these historic dry flies—and then tempting a beautiful trout to the surface. It's one of those incredibly fulfilling experiences in trout fly fishing. Give it a try.

CHAPTER 27

NORTH COUNTRY SPIDERS—CLASSIC SOFT HACKLES

Classic North Country spiders are wet flies that are incredibly simple impersonators of emergent aquatic insects. Even with a very modest fly form, these flies can create such lifelike movement in the water that they will often attract a hungry trout's eye much better than more anatomically precise imitations. The North Country spider is the forerunner of the dry fly for tempting trout to rise to the water surface to take emergent aquatic insects.

Here in North America, most trout flyfishers and fly tiers know these spider wet flies as "soft hackles" and may not be aware of their history and uses. In 1886, Englishman T. E. Pritt was one of the first to write about spider design in his publication *North Country Flies*, referring to a region in England where most streams are high-gradient, freestone waters. The term *spider* was, and is still, used in Great Britain in the same way North Americans use the terms *insects* or *bugs*. So, their popular British name "North Country spiders" is not intended to mean that these are actual imitations of arachnids (spiders). In 1981, Sylvester Nemes wrote his informative book *The Soft-Hackled Fly Addict*, revisiting soft hackles after he discovered how effective they were on US and Canadian trout streams. Most of us who tie and fish soft hackles today do so because of Sylvester's relentless endorsements of these amazing little wet flies and the unexpected results we enjoy with these tiny, extrasparse morsels.

The classic North Country spider is a strictly proportioned, sparsely constructed fly tied with just one or two turns of soft bird feather at the head and a slim thread, herl, or fur body. No wings, tail, sparkle, or added weighting. The soft feather barbules are believed to suggest the living movements, markings, and colors of an emerging aquatic insect's legs and wings, especially those of mayflies, caddis flies, and *diptera*.

Historically, tiers used the soft body plumage of game and songbirds, but today most songbirds and endangered game birds are protected and not available to fly tiers. The most popular hackle feathers for these spiders now are Hungarian partridge, grouse, snipe, quail, woodcock, hen chicken, sparrow, and starling. To expand the limited color ranges of these feathers, companies such as Wapsi carefully overdye them in yellows, olives, golds, black, brown, and fluorescent UV colors. Some fly tiers and production companies

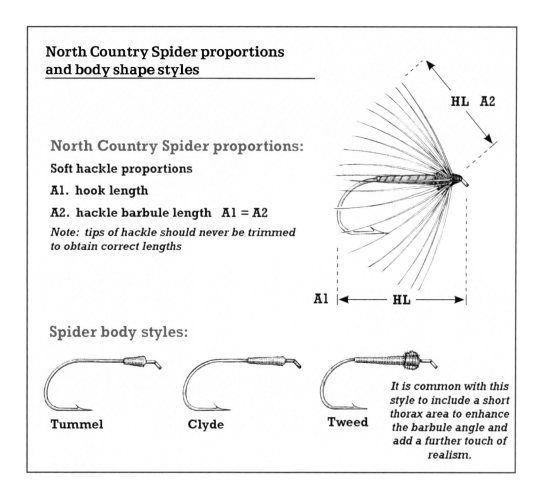

North Country Spider proportions and body shape styles

North Country Spider proportions:

Soft hackle proportions

A1. hook length

A2. hackle barbule length A1 = A2

Note: tips of hackle should never be trimmed to obtain correct lengths

HL A2

A1 HL

Spider body styles:

Tummel   Clyde   Tweed

It is common with this style to include a short thorax area to enhance the barbule angle and add a further touch of realism.

are modifying the soft-hackle spiders with glass and metal beads, wires, and flashy Mylar. When a fly is thus modified, it is no longer considered a true, classic spider, somewhat like adding lead wire to a dry fly. There is a growing popularity in dyeing soft hackle feathers with special fluorescent, UV-emitting colors. This seems, to some, to significantly improve trout numbers and size compared to natural colors. But, as Davy Wotton points out, the effectiveness of UV material is subject to many light and water conditions.

As an artist and tier, I am fascinated by the subtle but intricate pattern markings on soft hackle feathers, especially on Hungarian partridge, grouse, and bobwhite quail. Reproducing a soft-hackle texture, shape, and color pattern, using extrasharp colored pencils and very-fine ink pens, is quite a challenge—one that I simply love. While drawing, I like to envision a keen-eyed brown being triggered to rise and eat when, say, a partridge-and-orange spider's delicately moving image drifts into its feeding lane.

Feathers and North Country Spiders (opposite page).

Feathers (clockwise from top center): bobwhite quail (breast), cock pheasant (back), Hungarian partridge (breast), English sparrow (back), hen gamecock (back, dark ginger), hen gamecock (back, coch y bonddu), blue quail (flank), male starling (neck), Hungarian partridge (back).

Flies (clockwise): Pale Morning Dun, Hare's Lug, Partridge & Yellow, Waterhen Bloa, Grouse & Green, Spanish Needle, Blue Winged Olive, Black Spider; and (center) Partridge & Orange.

A group of lovely and typically sparse North Country spiders consisting of only one or two turns of soft, bird-body feathers and a sparse body of thread or fur dubbing.

As I was consulting with Davy Wotton about these North Country spiders, patterns he grew up using in Wales and regularly with success in the United States, he emphasized that they are most effective when fished on short, upstream casts and precisely drifted with the least drag possible, quite similar to presenting a dry fly to a rise. That surprised me a bit because I, and others I've known, have done most of our soft-hackle fishing with a subtle, across-and-down drift. Davy correctly reminded me that these flies were developed to take trout feeding on near-surface drifting emergers, not the fast-swimming or swinging aquatics or attractors that are more common with the traditional winged wet flies. This drift, using the natural current speed and direction, allows the soft legs to do their best, most intricate live dance.

When we lived near the White River and Norfork tailwaters in Arkansas, Davy gave me several simple, size 20 to 22 soft hackles that had thin, silver bodies and just one turn of dark dun starling feather each. Fished as he recommended, I was able to engage some very large trout below Bull Shoals dam on clear, low-water, and extra-smooth moderate flow rates. I drifted my copies of Davy's starling spiders to these big midging trout and became a real believer as I caught more with those flies than with my more imitative midge designs. It *had* to be the soft hackle barbule movement that attracted these spooky, superselective trophies.

The White River's eighty miles of trout stream below Bull Shoals dam may be the hardest fished of any of North America's trout rivers because everything is allowed: live bait, power bait, hardware, lures, and flies. Stocked rainbows and browns seldom survive this relentless pressure for more than a few weeks, and the monster wild browns that swim there have only survived by learning very selective feeding. A friend of mine, Tom Bullock, recently caught a thirty-inch brown using a size 14, partridge-and-orange spider. What could be better testimonial for these remarkable little flies?

Davy also recommends using a 10- or 11-foot, mid-flex, 3- or 4-weight rod, a dressed, high-floating double taper, hi-vis pastel or white fly line, and a leader attached with a Zap-A-Gap knotless connection—10 to 14 feet depending upon how many soft hackle are used at one time. This tackle gives superior short-distance, upstream presentations and best drift control, along with good sight and touch sensations for detecting the trout's take. If flies are close to the surface, these takes may be visual. A leader pause, twitch, swirl, or sharp pull are indicators if you can't see the take. The use of a small, neutral-colored yarn or cul de canard (CDC) locator is a significant aid for tracking spiders that are out of sight just under the surface, and for detecting strikes, especially when first starting to use these flies and this method. However, it usually doesn't take long for most folks to develop the focus and feel to sense the takes without these locators. In all cases, respond with a smooth, prompt, gentle lift of the rod tip to properly engage the hook. This is very similar to a midge strike. The nylon or fluorocarbon tippet should be 4X for fly sizes 10, 12, and 14; 5X for 14 to 18; and 6X for 18 to 22. If you use one or two dropper flies, tie them on a dropper length of 6 or 8 inches and about 24 to 30 inches apart. (Always check the regulations for number of flies allowed.) The double surgeon knot or blood knot is ideal for forming each tippet and dropper section.

With their small sizes, simplistic hackle volume, and sparse bodies, soft-hackle spiders are the perfect example of the least being the most! During sparse or significant emergences (or even no activity), a few simple, soft-hackle spiders presented and skillfully drifted have been for over two centuries—and is still today—an incredibly consistent way to take those elusive, selective trout. I hope you'll try "spider troutin'" this year. I'll bet you'll be, as I was, very pleasantly surprised and rewarded. May the soft hackles entice some very special trout to rise to your fly.

For much more information about these most interesting flies, please read *The North Country Fly: Yorkshire's Soft Hackle Tradition*, by Robert L. Smith (Coch-y-Bonddu Books, 2015).

Soft feathers, such as this Hungarian partridge feather, make the most ideal hackle for North Country Spiders— often known as soft hackles in the United States. These feathers have soft, webby barbules that make each spider sink easily and have the natural, water-swimming movements of live, aquatic insects. Beautiful colors and intricate markings mimic realism even further to the trout's eye.

CHAPTER 28

THE CLASSIC TROUT FISHER'S NYMPH

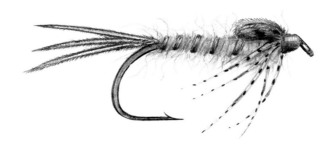

The nymph fly was originally considered an imitation of the immature phase of Ephemeroptera (mayflies). Developed in Europe during the late 1800s and early 1900s, G. E. M. Skues is most credited with the first impressionistic nymphal flies and the initial methods of fishing them for trout in England's southern chalk and limestone streams. Skues's observations of feeding trout and study of their stomach contents led him to correctly believe that trout feed most consistently on subsurface food forms day-to-day, month-to-month, and season-to-season. Many decades later, this method would eventually replace surface fly fishing for trout in popularity and effectiveness both on the European continent and in the United States. It's often said that Skues's first nymph book, *Minor Tactics of the Chalk Stream (1914)*, should be retitled *Major Tactics for Trout*.

Although Skues's work received the most recognition, others in that period were contributing to the development of imitating subsurface insects and invertebrates. A "Dr. Bell" was paralleling Skues's line of reasoning on English still waters, but Bell was imitating immature chironomids (midges) and sedges (caddis flies). Bell

developed the midge emerger Bell's Buzzer and the caddis emerger known as the Amber Nymph.

Skues and the nymphing method he developed came under much criticism from the many dry-fly purists who believed that fishing a fly below the surface was almost sacrilege, especially from those privileged few who were members of exclusive fly-fishing clubs or royalty-owned chalk streams. The fly-fishing literature then and in the twentieth century has humorous and not-so-humorous stories about flyfishers who were caught fishing *below the surface* on these sacred dry-fly waters. Even today such subsurface trout flies are restricted on certain private trout waters.

Skues and one of his most respected nymph-fly disciples, Frank Sawyer, believed that only the abundant, swimming mayfly nymphs found in chalk streams were practical to imitate. As you can see in my illustrations, Skues's and Sawyer's favorite nymph patterns were *very* simple, impressionistic designs. When these flies and nymphing technique came to America, they were unpopular and relatively ineffective because our trout waters (especially in the East) consist of streams that are very different from the English

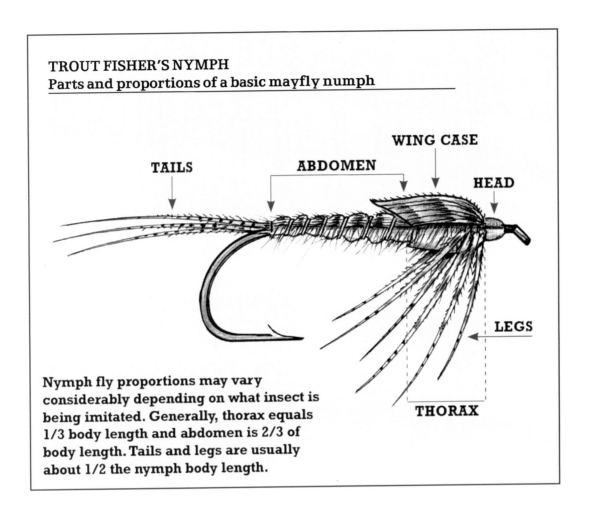

TROUT FISHER'S NYMPH
Parts and proportions of a basic mayfly numph

TAILS

ABDOMEN

WING CASE

HEAD

LEGS

THORAX

Nymph fly proportions may vary considerably depending on what insect is being imitated. Generally, thorax equals 1/3 body length and abdomen is 2/3 of body length. Tails and legs are usually about 1/2 the nymph body length.

chalk streams. Likewise, these early nymph flies were not good imitations of the varieties of burrowing and crawling mayflies, stoneflies, and other immature aquatic insects that occur in our freestone streams.

The American nymph hybridization of the first European nymphs, along with a limited knowledge of the structure, texture, and living modes of the various important species, produced a series of nymphal designs that were quite unrealistic. I've included illustrations from some of the early American tiers: Hewitt, Burke, and Bergman. The result was a period of nymphal imitation limbo until the mid-twentieth century, when improv-

The first three historic eras of nymphs (opposite page, left to right from top).

Top 5—Samples of earliest nymph fly development. G. E. M. Skue's Medium Olive Dun, Blue Wing Olive, Iron Blue Dun; Frank Sawyer's Gray Goose, Pheasant Tail Nymph.

Middle 4—Early North American nymphs. George Hewitt: Flat-Bodied Nymph; Ray Bergman: No. 1 RB Translucent Green Nymph; Ed Burke's Nymph.

Bottom 10—Third-era nymph flies. Art Flick: March Brown; John Atherton: No. 3 Dark Nymph; Doug Prince: Prince Nymph, Gold Ribbed Hare's Ear; Polly Rosborough: Damsel Nymph; Dave Whitlock: Red Fox Squirrel Nymph, S & R Hexagenia Wiggle Nymph; Randall Kaufman: Black Stone; Andy Puyans: Black Beaver Nymph; Al Troth: Pheasant Tail Nymph.

Gold-Ribbed Hare's Ear

Whitlock's Red Fox Squirrel Nymph

ing entomological knowledge of aquatic insects began to inspire such notable angler-tiers as Art Flick, Polly Rosborough, Al Troth, George Grant, John Atherton, Al McClane, Ted Trueblood, Doug Prince, Doug Swisher, Carl Richards, Al Caucci, Randall Kaufman, Bob Nastasi, Andy Puyans, myself, and others to create imitations that looked, felt, and fished like the major, nymphal aquatic insects across North America. Nymphing here also became easier and more popular after I developed and wrote about the strike indicator.

The successful nymph flies of this time had several things in common: they were impressionistic and had the correct sizes, color patterns, and densities to attract trout in streams throughout North and South America. Many of these flies were, and continue to be, extremely successful at enticing trout. Early on, most were mayfly and stonefly imitations. Caddis and midges, whose early life forms are sometimes referred to

as nymphs, have a larva and pupa stage instead of a nymphal form and so were not considered for imitating by most. I'll cover caddis and midge flies in a later chapter.

Although modern fly-tying materials and techniques allow tiers to sculpture nymph imitations that look precisely like the live forms, these beautiful, time-consuming imitations are often not as effective at catching trout. Just last summer I tested some of the most realistic stonefly nymphs I'd ever seen, along with my favorite impressionistic stonefly nymphs, on the Madison and Yellowstone Rivers. My success ratio was always better when using the impressionistic imitations.

As I see it, there are four generations of nymph flies: those very sparsely-tied, impressionistic nymphs from the Skues and Sawyer era; the unrealistic early American nymphs; nymphs from the mid-to-end of the twentieth century, tied mainly with soft, natural materials such as feathers and animal fur dubbings; and then those of this current era, which tend to be constructed of hard, brightly colored materials and metallic beads.

Trout nymphing in North America is, in my estimation, the most effective, complex, and popular way to fly fish for trout. I'd like to recommend readers to find a copy of *Masters on the Nymph* by J. Michael and Leonard Wright Jr., illustrated by Dave Whitlock (Lyons Press, 1979 [out of print]). It features an amazing lineup of now-historic, twentieth-century experts, who accurately capture the full essence and scope of the nymph fly's creation, development, and popularity in our sport of fly fishing for trout.

Our sport may be aging, but many of the classic nymph designs of the last seventy-five years are ageless and still produce very good results.

CHAPTER 29

CLASSIC FEATHERED TROUT STREAMERS

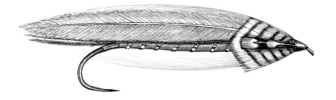

The streamer fly is a long-bodied design that imitates small forage fish that are prey for trout, char, and landlocked salmon. These streamers were developed to catch larger trout that feed on quantities of minnows, trout parr, and other small fish as the trout mature and require more food intake in order to continue growing.

There is evidence that streamer lures were used by nonflyfishers in ancient Macedonia and by early Alaskan Eskimos, but the design is first known in North America from the very late 1800s. It is recorded in our fly-fishing literature that around 1890–1901, Herbert L. Welch, of Mooselookmeguntic, Maine, tied some of the first true streamer flies to imitate forage fish that occur in the northeastern waters of the United States. His flies—Welch Rarebit, Black Ghost, Jane Craig, Green Spot, and Welch Montreal— were apparently all very effective in the early 1900s and remain as classic, popular streamers today.

Welch was one of the first American flyfishers to realize that the diets of larger trout, char, and landlocks contained significant amounts of small fishes. Another streamer tier from Maine, Carrie Stevens (1882–1970), gets my vote for fashioning the most perfectly tied feather streamers. Her streamers stand alone for their design precision, material proportions, and colorations, as well as their classic effectiveness and lasting popularity. I've included some of

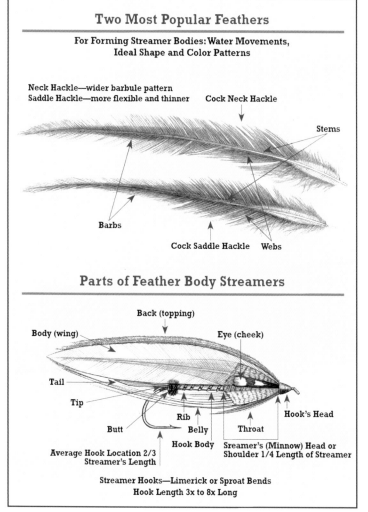

Two Most Popular Feathers

For Forming Streamer Bodies: Water Movements, Ideal Shape and Color Patterns

Neck Hackle—wider barbule pattern
Saddle Hackle—more flexible and thinner
Cock Neck Hackle
Stems
Barbs
Cock Saddle Hackle   Webs

Parts of Feather Body Streamers

Back (topping)
Body (wing)
Eye (cheek)
Tail
Tip
Rib
Hook's Head
Butt
Belly
Throat
Hook Body
Average Hook Location 2/3 Streamer's Length
Sreamer's (Minnow) Head or Shoulder 1/4 Length of Streamer

Streamer Hooks—Limerick or Sproat Bends
Hook Length 3x to 8x Long

her streamers in the illustration. Carrie's "Gray Ghost" is said to be the best-known streamer fly throughout the fly-fishing world.

A close second for creating especially high-quality and beautiful streamers was Lew Oatman (1902–1959). Lew's Brook Trout, Male Dace, and Silver Darter are illustrated here, and one look will convince even the most critical eye that his work is pure classical excellence!

I was pleasantly surprised to learn, during my streamer history search, that Theodore Gordon had also created early streamers, although not initially for trout. His designs were to lure in pike, bass, and perch. However, his Bumblepuppy streamer was eventually proven to be an excellent brown and brook trout fly, especially in low-visibility waters and at night. It continues to appear on the "favorite fly lists" of many writers, even today.

Feather-bodied streamers for trout are usually constructed on long-shank, Limerick- or Sproat-bend hooks in sizes 10 to 1/0. The most popular are those that are 2 to 4 inches long. The hook point is located at about two-thirds the length of the body. Tandem hooks in the midbody and at the very tail are sometimes tied into streamers that are to be trolled or used to hook fish that tend to strike at a streamer's tail. The body feathers, originally called wings, are usually best constructed from cock necks or saddle hackles that are thin-stemmed and have a moderate-to-wide-width web to give the fly the ideal fish shape and movement in the water. For the streamers with darker backs, peacock or ostrich herl are most ideal, and the flexibility of these feather strands complements the desired body movement of these flies.

Around 1975, Dave Inks and Doug Swisher introduced the New Zealand "Matuka" method for creating the body of the streamer. I've always felt that this method is incredibly effective for streamer shape and water performance; plus, this

Classic feathered trout streamers (opposite page).

Welch Rarebit—Originated by Herbert L Welch, this fly is often credited as the first streamer for trout and landlocked salmon (1902).

Black Ghost—Originated by "Herbie" Welch, it is still one of the most well-known streamers.

Bumblepuppy—Originated by Theodore Gordon around 1880. First tied as a pike fly, it eventually evolved into a very popular brown and brook trout night fly.

Don's Delight—by Carrie Stevens.

Gray Ghost—Originated by Carrie Stevens, it may be the best-known streamer across the trout and salmon world.

Ebden's Fancy—A Carrie Stevens original, it is a classic example of blending several hackle markings and colors to achieve an overall natural color pattern.

Male Dace—by Lew Oatman.

Brook Trout—by Lew Oatman.

Silver Darter—by Lew Oatman.

Nine Three (tied tandem)—Originated by Dr. Hubert Sanborn to imitate smelt.

Supervisor Imperial (tied tandem)—by Warden Supervisor Joseph S. Stickney in Saco, Maine, to imitate finger smelt.

Matuka—The Matuka is one of the many uniquely formed flies from New Zealand.

Matuka Silver Spruce—by Dave Whitlock.

Olive "Green Machine" Matuka—by Doug Swisher. An outstanding searching, attractor streamer.

Little Brown Trout—by Dave Whitlock: Match-the-Minnow series.

Shad Alewife—by Dave Whitlock: Match-the-Minnow series.

Yellow Perch—by Dave Whitlock: Match-the-Minnow series.

Silver Minnow "The Incredible"—by Al Giradot. A perennial classic feather-bodied streamer.

Pink Lady—by Carrie Stevens. A most beautiful classic streamer to complete this illustration, as it was Carrie's last streamer she tied, finished with a gold-thread head ring on December 4, 1953.

technique helps prevent the tangling of the back feathers around the hook when cast. To imitate the coloration and markings of natural foods, badger, cree, furnace, chinchilla, and grizzly hackles are unsurpassed. When carefully dyed or overlaid with other hackle colors, remarkably beautiful minnow body imitations are possible. Marabou feathers and ostrich and peacock herls can be used to simulate the lower belly and further enhance realism and swimming movement. The hackle stem admirably depicts the lateral line that all small fishes have along their sides from head to tail. Because predators are particularly triggered to attack prey when eye contact is made, most streamers are adorned with a pair of vivid eyes on their heads. The gorgeous, spotted neck feathers of the jungle cock are the classic feathers for eyes, but being endangered, this once-wild game bird is now pen-raised, and the feathers are expensive. A number of realistic jungle cock imitations, paints, and plastic eyes have become available and are widely accepted by today's streamer tiers and fishers.

Most small fish that trout feed on, such as shiners, dace, chubs, shad, smelt and trout parr, display light reflective side scales, especially when they are actively feeding or injured. Highly reflective metallic and pearlescent Mylar strands, such as Flashabou and Crystal Flash, incorporated into the streamer fly complete the illusion of the live minnow. These graceful, long, slender flies, with their intricate coloring and neatly proportioned feather bodies, captivate both trout and the flyfisher's eyes. I love the challenge of illustrating these little works of art with my paints and pencils as much as sculpting them at my tying desk.

In my lifetime, I've watched streamers become even more effective as weights such as split shot, lead wire, metal beads, dumbbell eyes, and tungsten cones have become legal and accepted by flyfishers. Sinking tip and full-sinking lines can further enhance the ability to reach swifter and deeper trout waters. Unlike most aquatic invertebrate imitations that should be fished with very precise water action, streamers are effective when worked up, down, or across-stream as long as one is imitating the action of minnows that are fleeing, feeding, disabled, or swimming. Quick directional changes, erratic pauses, and twitches often trigger a trout's predator instincts to attack the streamer. Actually, these unique, animating lure movements are only possible with a fly line and rod. Joe Brooks, a devoted trout-streamer expert, often said that streamers worked best in current when presented so the trout could see a side view, and in still waters when swum directly by a trout's nose. I often hear streamer flyfishers remark that working streamers in flowing and still waters is much more proactive and interesting than drifting insect imitations down current. I, myself, love them both.

A good assortment of productive feather-bodied streamers should match the sizes of minnows that trout feed on; have the color, shape, and action of the naturals; and be impressionistic rather than an exact imitation. Try to add some black, white, and fluorescent color patterns to your fly box for when water visibility is limited by murkiness or low-light conditions.

As with most flies, streamer designs are continually evolving as our knowledge, materials, and methods are expanding, but the classic feather-bodied streamers still have an important place in your fly box.

For further reading and tying methods, see:
Stream Fly Tying and Fishing by Joseph D. Bates Jr. (Stackpole Books, 1966).
The Founding Flies by Mike Valle (Stackpole Books, 2013).

CHAPTER 30

CLASSIC TERRESTRIAL FLIES

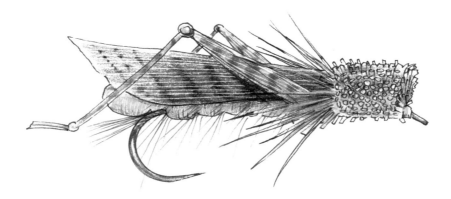

Terrestrial insects are land-born, air-breathing insects that become important for flyfishers when they accidentally land or fall on a water surface. Trout will enthusiastically feed on them, especially during late summer through fall when there are usually more terrestrials than aquatic insects in and on the water.

In the late nineteenth and early twentieth centuries, American trout flyfishers (especially those in the Northeast) began to see the purity of their trout streams being compromised. Because aquatic insect numbers were most affected by this water-quality degradation, these flyfishers gradually became more aware of the importance of terrestrial insects for trout, so they started developing fly designs that imitated ants, beetles, leaf hoppers, grasshoppers, crickets, and caterpillars.

The stream and spring creek regions of Michigan and Pennsylvania were especially prominent in a revolutionary American movement of terrestrial trout fly designs and how to fish them. I first learned of terrestrials for trout in the 1950s from the books and magazine features of Vince Marinaro, Charlie Fox, Ed Shenk, and

Chauncy Lively. Like many flyfishers at the time, I was rather intimidated by the mystery of matching the hatches and spinner falls of all those Latin-named aquatic insects. It was great news when I learned that plain old "bugs" would also catch trout. These pioneering men each spent many seasons on spring creeks observing selective trout-feeding behavior. Terrestrials helped them solve many of the selective-feeding codes of trout! I particularly admired Chauncy Lively's series in *Pennsylvania Anglers,* as he always had such cool and interesting perspectives about tying and fishing terrestrial imitations.

As the name implies, terrestrial insects are supposed to live on land and are not well suited for time in water, only ending up there accidentally when they are blown in, knocked in, or because of some other mishap. A few terrestrial insects, such as moths, wasps, and bees, will light temporarily on the water's surface for a quick drink. A well-designed terrestrial imitation should not only resemble the naturals, but be constructed to strike the water surface with a *plop* sound that resembles the impact these terrestrials make when

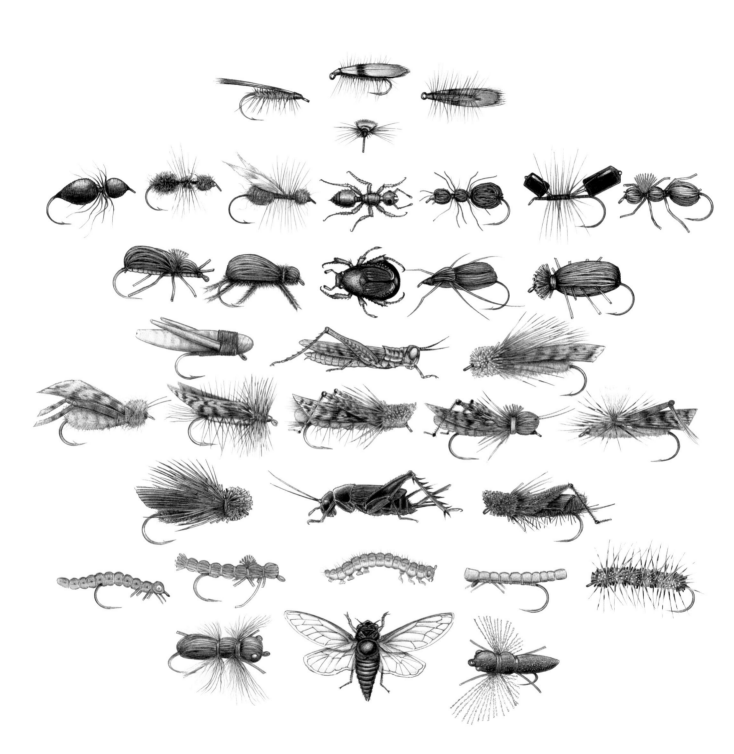

they crash or fall into the water. It should also float very low in the water surface film or sink a bit just like the fallen naturals do. However, because any low-floating fly is difficult to see, they work best for the flyfisher when tied with a small, bright bit of color somewhere on the top of the fly. When tying my own flies, I use a small fluorescent tuft of yarn or foam on top of the thorax. I call these flies bright- or hot-spot imitations. They are much easier to spot when cast, which in turn allows for a quicker hook set and increased takes.

Because terrestrials are usually mature and very active during the warmest times of the summer and fall, they are unintentionally in contact with the water most often at that time of year. It also happens that most aquatic insect hatches are over for the season and not available to trout on a regular basis, making terrestrials a very important food source. There is, however, a type of terrestrial that is eagerly accepted almost any time of year, even amidst aquatic insect hatches—small black ants or beetles. When I just can't seem to match a hatch effectively, I will often place a small, black imitation on my tippet. I can't tell you how often this has brought about immediate success floating this little bug among the duns or spinners. According to reports, trout have a kind of "sour tooth" for the formic acid, tart taste of ants. They also can't seem to resist a size 12 to 24 black silhouette stuck in the surface film.

Most classic terrestrials are constructed with natural materials, such as deer, elk, and moose body hair—with versatile elk hair being the favorite. These coarse, buoyant hairs, when over-coated with flexible transparent cement, are durable, float well, and make very realistic-looking bugs. Bird wing and tail feather quills are also excellent for constructing low-floating terrestrial wing covers, bodies, and appendages. Balsa, cork, and molded foam rubber are also useful. Over the last couple of decades, foam-rubber sheets and cylinders, rubber strand legs, wildly colored poly yarns, and iridescent, metallic Mylars have become very popular for creating all sorts of sur-realistic, attractor terrestrials. The more realistic, classic terrestrials I've chosen to illustrate are

(Opposite page.)

Top four flies: Jassids

Row 2: Ants

    1. Enameled Wet Ant.

    2. Fur Ant.

    3. Cinnamon Flying Ant.

    4. Deer Hair Carpenter Ant—designed by Chauncy Lively.

    5. McMurry Ant—designed by Ed Sutryn.

    6. Bright-Spot Elk Hair Ant—designed by Dave Whitlock.

Row 3: Beetles

    1. Bright-Spot Elk Hair Beetle—designed by Dave Whitlock.

    2. Shenk's Beetle—designed by Ed Shenk.

    3. Quill-Back Beetle—by Chauncy Lively.

    4. Crowe Beetle—by John Crowe.

Row 4: Grasshoppers

    1. Pontoon Hopper—by Vince Marinaro.

    2. Letort Hopper—by Ed Shenk.

Row 5: Grasshoppers

    1. Sunken Hopper—by Ed Shenk.

    2. Joe's Hopper—by Art Winnie.

    3. Dave's Hopper—by Dave Whitlock.

    4. Whit Hopper—by Dave Whitlock.

    5. Parachute Hopper—by Ed Schroeder.

Row 6: Crickets

    1. Letort Cricket—by Ed Shenk.

    2. Dave's Cricket—by Dave Whitlock.

Row 7: Caterpillars

    1. Green Inchworm.

    2. Bright-Spot Inchworm—by Dave Whitlock.

    3. Foam Green Cylinder Worm.

    4. Fuzzy Deer Hair Caterpillar.

Row 8: Cicadas

    1. Spent Elk Hair Cicada.

    2. Whitlock Crystal Flash Spent Cicada—by Dave Whitlock.

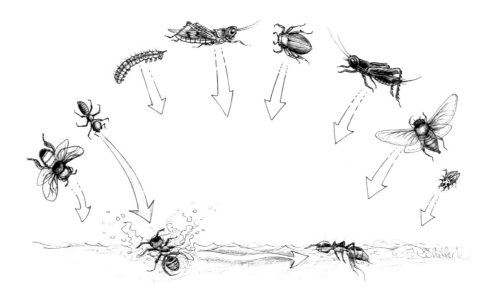

Land-born, air-breathing insects are an important source of food for trout. They unintentionally fall or crash into the water and usually make a splashy *plop* sound and then float low in the surface. The flyfisher that mimics this sound and drift can experience some very exciting summer and fall fishing.

both of historic and more modern designs, and I feel they should always have a dedicated place in your box of terrestrials.

Don't hesitate to use them from May to November, especially on warm and windy days when you encounter a meadow or forested border along a stream you are fishing. Whether your trout sips or slams your bug, terrestrials always make for another dimension of unforgettable trout fishing.

For more precise information on classic terrestrials, I recommend:

Tying and Fishing Terrestrials by Gerald Almy (Stackpole Books, 1978).

The Founding Flies, by Mike Valla (Stackpole Books, 2013).

A Modern Dry Fly Code by Vince Marinaro (Echo Point Books & Media, 2015).

Rising Trout by Charley Fox (Dutton Adult, 1978).

Trout and Their Food by Dave Whitlock (Skyhorse Publishing, 2010).

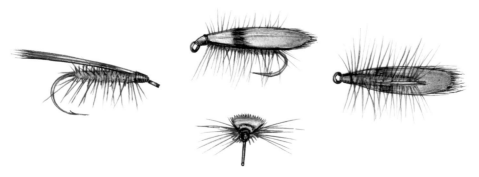

The Jassid was originated by Vincent C Marinaro to imitate beetles, leaf hoppers, and jassids.

CHAPTER 31

CLASSIC MIDGES

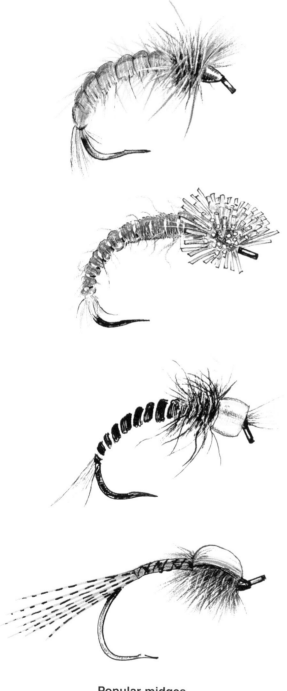

Popular midges.

The midge fly is an imitation of a two-winged, nonbiting insect that resembles a mosquito and can be so small that ten to twelve will fit comfortably on the face of a dime. The Chironomidae family represents a huge group in the Diptera order, which includes crane flies, blackflies, deerflies, and mosquitos. Imitating midges did not begin in earnest until the early 1900s, when flyfishers in Europe began fishing midge-laden reservoirs. North American midging developed even later, as huge populations of midges became apparent in our lakes, reservoirs, and tailwaters. Because of their generally small sizes (18 to 28), precise midge techniques and flies became practical for the general public only when new, lighter-weight rod, line, and leader technology enabled trout flyfishers to present and fish midge imitations effectively.

Midges are very abundant in most trout streams and still waters, often exceeding any other aquatic invertebrate by total weight of food annually available to trout. It's sometimes hard to realize that adult trout, grayling, char, and whitefish all eagerly feed on insects and crustaceans that are one-sixteenth of an inch and smaller. Being able to tie and fish the tiny midges on which trout are feeding enables us to reach, in my opinion, fly fishing's ultimate level of refinement . . . such as using a size 24 midge on a 7X tippet and 1- to-3-weight rod to catch a twenty-four-inch trout!

The midge's life cycle, similar to caddis, has four phases—egg, larva, pupa, and adult—and

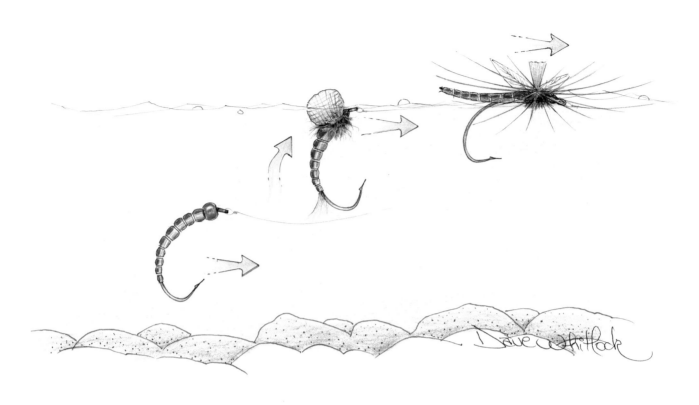

1. Larva: Fish larvae close to bottom of stream or still water. 2. Pupa. 2a. Emerging: Make pupa swim or drift up to surface. 2b. Below surface film: Pupa should suspend vertically by using buoyant tying material. 3. Midge adult: Fish in surface film.

Classic midge designs (opposite page).

Top row: Early midge flies
    1. Bell's Buzzer (mid-1900s)
    2. Goddard's Suspender Buzzer—John Goddard (1960s)
    3. Midge Pupa (mid-1900s)
Row 2: Adults
    1. Conover's Clumper—Griffith's Gnat
    2. Adult Midge
    3. Monopost Para-Midge—Dave Whitlock
Row 3: Surface film emergent pupa
    1. Stillborn Midge—Carl Richards

    2. Midge Pupa
    3. Serendipity—Ross Marigold (subsurface and surface film)
Row 4: Subsurface pupa and Larva
    1. Starling and Silver Midge Spider—Davy Wotton
    2. Larva Lace Pupa Buzzer
    3. Larva
    4. Brassie—Lynch, Chandler and Davenport
Row 5: Subsurface pupa and larva
    1. Glass bead pupa—Dave Whitlock
    2. Larva Lace Blood-Worm larva
    3. Bead-Head Zebra Midge—Pat Dorsey

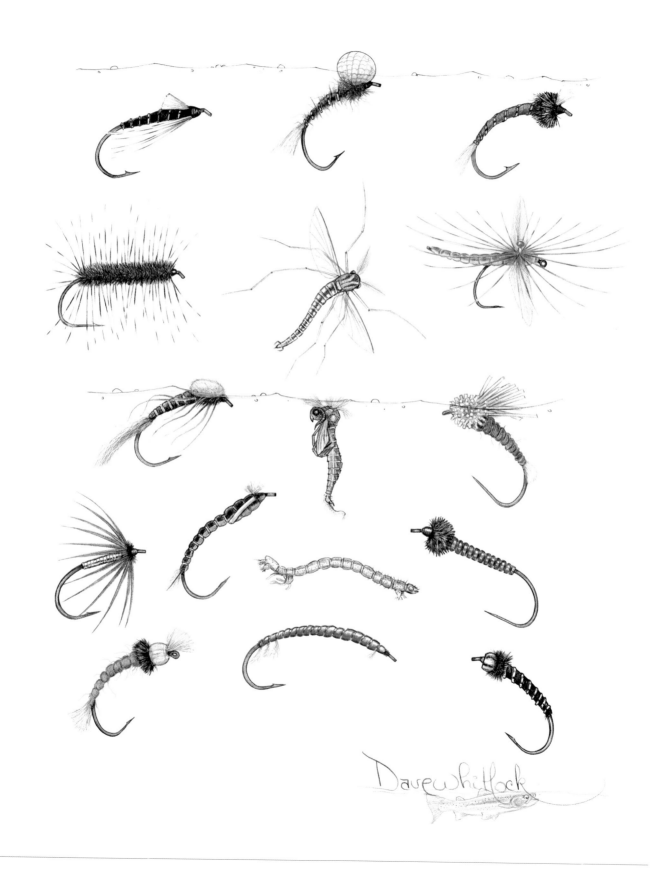

Dave Whitlock

can produce as many as four generations per year, although the average is two. They can tolerate a wide range of water and air temperatures, and so even late in fall, winter, and early spring, surface midging can be incredible below tailwaters, and on spring creeks and unfrozen ponds and lakes.

The most popular midge form to imitate is the emergent pupa. Pupas slowly swim upward to the surface, suspending in the surface film for a while before splitting their pupal skins and emerging as air-breathing, flying adults. Trout usually take their time feeding with open mouths on these surface-emergent pupae—taking in a mouthful, going down to swallow, and then back up for more. It is mesmerizing to watch, and fishing to these slow-moving feeders can truly challenge your best skills of delicate and accurate presentation, perfect drag-free drifts, subtle strike detection, and delicate hook sets. I often describe this hook set as what you'd do to tighten your leader if it was strand of spider web. Most often, the tiny hooks stick just in the skin of the lip or mouth and can be pulled out fairly easily if not gently handled.

Midge fly imitations are usually tied on extra-short-shank, barbless hooks, providing a relatively wider gape and stronger hook to cope with the challenge of hooking and holding large trout during extralong battles. Body materials such as soft, fine-textured dubbing, CDC, marabou, ostrich, peacock herl, and soft hackle make the most realistically textured midges. Adding wire, thread, and beads to midge flies is also popular.

The larvae and emerging pupae are almost impossible to see on or below the water, and I usually recommend some form of small yarn or CDC locator to see the fly's location and detect the strike. The little indicators that I use are about the size of a BB.

When first learning to midge fish, flyfishers often tie a small, colorful bead/wire attractor midge to a larger fly such as a hopper, streamer, or nymph using 8 to 12 inches of 4X tippet and 4- to 6-weight rods.

This will definitely catch trout. But as skills increase, so can the fly-fishing challenge and enjoyment. I wholeheartedly recommend improving your skills to the point of using flies that closely match the size and color of the emerging midges with a tiny indicator and fishing them on very lightweight tackles, mainly 1- or 2-weight rods, attached to 10 to 16 feet of 6X to 8X tippet. Delicately presented to specific risers, even a fourteen-inch trout becomes a challenge, and a twenty-incher on a size 22 midge and 2-weight rod will be an unforgettable experience. It's somewhat like taming a tiger with a whip and a chair. If a higher plane of delicate fly fishing exists, I'm not aware of it.

What we call the classic midge flies are actually fairly modern, compared to other fly designs. I've illustrated a selection of them that represents both historic and current midge flies to give you an enlarged perspective of midges. If you haven't midge fished yet, give it a try; you may just fall in love with it just like Em and I have.

CHAPTER 32

CLASSIC BUCKTAIL STREAMERS

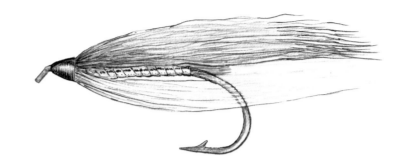

Bucktail streamers are imitations of small fish that are fed upon by predator fish. The bucktail's most distinguishing characteristic is the hair from which the body is constructed—frequently long, tapering, crinkly hair from the tail of a whitetail buck deer. However, other long hair, such as polar bear, foxtail, goat, Icelandic sheep, raccoon, and squirrel tail is often used with excellent results.

The bucktail streamer is a relatively recent contribution to trout fly fishing, but crude hair streamers were used centuries ago by various indigenous tribes, who constructed them by attaching long animal hair to bone and wooden hooks. Around 1875 here in North America, warmwater flyfishers began using hair to make long-bodied flies to imitate small fish to catch bass, pike, and saltwater fishes. Originally and traditionally, the materials tied at the head of a streamer were called "wings," but they actually form the major portion of the streamer's body. Eventually, hair streamer designs were adopted by trout flyfishers.

I mentioned in the feather streamer chapter how Theodore Gordon, the "Father of American dry-fly fishing" was one of the first streamer pioneers. His famous Bumblepuppy streamer can be classified with the feather streamers and

with the bucktails because it was tied using both materials. Initially created around 1880 to catch bass and pike, by 1903 his design was being used very effectively to catch large trout, especially at night. In 1875, Harvey A. Donaldson, a New York firearms expert and renowned flyfisher, began tying some of the first bicolor bucktail streamers, using brown and white bucktail hair. Around 1900, Carter Harrison, one-time mayor of Chicago, in jest created a hair streamer using hair from a red spaniel and wool from a handy red rug. He was staying at the A. S. Trude Ranch in Idaho at the time and so named it the Trude Bucktail. However, because it looked and worked so well, it was later modified using easier-to-obtain red fox squirrel tail hair for the body and red wool yarn for the body ribbed with flat silver. William Scripture Jr. of New York created the all-brown Scripture Bucktail in 1907. Soon after this, Maine and New England trout flyfishers and guides began to see the incredible effectiveness and durability of bucktail streamers and so spread the word. Over the years, from its humble, warmwater beginnings, bucktail streamers have continued to become more and more popular with trout flyfishers, especially those seeking big trout and char.

ARTFUL PROFILES

Initially, hair streamers were constructed very simply. A hank of long hair was tied to the hook just past the eye and extended back a full hook length beyond the hook bend. Early on, the hair was usually white and was accented by silver tinsel wrapped over the hook shank to the bend. A short, colorful tuft of wool or feather (most often red) was added just forward of the hook bend. One hindrance for fly tiers at the time was the shortage of hooks that were long enough. Longer hooks could be made by hand, and eventually hooks became available from manufacturers. As time passed, in order to more closely imitate baitfish color patterns, various hair colors and markings were stacked on the hook to look more like naturals. Later, gills, eyes, and reflective strands were added to further perfect the realism. The eyed feathers from jungle cock were an important component of many of the early designs, but as these feathers became scarce and illegal, we began painting the eyes on the head thread wraps or on the absorbent cheek feather. Because these paint spots seldom looked realistic, I began to explore other eye substitutes, and in 1968, I found what I was looking for: plastic doll eyes that could be glued to the fly head. They looked and worked great! So much so that now there is a whole spectrum of streamer eyes that will match any baitfish color and size one can imagine.

This bucktail streamer's effectiveness can be greatly improved by using sinking-tip and full-sinking lines, lead wire, dumbbell lead eyes, metal cone heads, and metal beads, particularly when streams are fast, at high levels, larger, or when going for trout, char, and salmon in deep lakes. The type of movement imparted to these baitfish imitations can also increase success rates, especially if the fly appears to be distressed or wounded. Such movements can really trigger a big, predator trout strike. Puppeteering a bucktail streamer—using rod tip movements, line strips and pauses, and mending the line right and left to change swimming directions—makes a bucktail come to life when detected by the eyes, lateral line, and inner ear of a hungry trout.

Over the last seventy-five years, as trout have become more selective, bucktail streamers have evolved from basic white hair and silver tinsel to much more attractive and realistic color and shape patterns. First, various hair colors were used, followed by specific minnow body parts, such as eyes, gills, scales, fins and tails, making bucktail streamers look more appealing to flyfishers and hopefully to those largest of selective trout. Annually, new synthetic hair, specialized dying and marking methods to add spots, bands, and bars to streamer hair, UV/fluorescent colors, and seemingly limitless product lists of reflec-

Classic Bucktail Streamers (opposite page):

From the top down, left to right.

1. Early, simplistic white and silver bucktail streamer (1800s).
2. Bumblepuppy—Theodore Gordon (1880).
3. Brown and White Bucktail—Harvey Donaldson (1875).
4. Scripture Bucktail—William E. Scripture Jr. (1907).
5. Mickey Finn—John Alden Knight (1937).
6. Trude Bucktail (using fox squirrel)—Carter Harrison (1900).
7. Shushan Postmaster—Lew Oatman (1956).
8. Little Brook Trout Bucktail—Samuel Slaymaker II (1976).
9. Thunder Creek Silver Shiner—Keith Fulsher (1962).

10. Red Shiner Bucktail—Helen Shaw (1968).
11. Black Nose Dace Bucktail—Art Flick (1960).
12. Llama Bucktail (woodchuck hair)—popularized by Eric Leiser.
13. Zonker—Dan Byford and Leatherneck Chauncy Lively (1981).
14. Integration Bucktail—Ted Trueblood.
15. Polly's Polar Chub—Polly Rosborough (1955).
16. Platinum Blonde—Joe Brooks (1939).
17. Clouser Bucktail Minnow—Bob Clouser.
18. Swimming Sheep Minnow—Dave Whitlock (1990).
19. Mega Articulated Bucktail—various designs by Kelly Gallop, Dave Whitlock, Pat Ehlers.

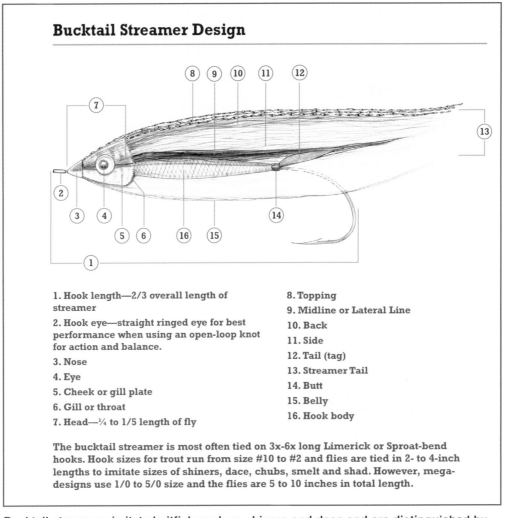

Bucktail Streamer Design

1. **Hook length—2/3 overall length of streamer**
2. **Hook eye—straight ringed eye for best performance when using an open-loop knot for action and balance.**
3. **Nose**
4. **Eye**
5. **Cheek or gill plate**
6. **Gill or throat**
7. **Head—¼ to 1/5 length of fly**

8. **Topping**
9. **Midline or Lateral Line**
10. **Back**
11. **Side**
12. **Tail (tag)**
13. **Streamer Tail**
14. **Butt**
15. **Belly**
16. **Hook body**

The bucktail streamer is most often tied on 3x-6x long Limerick or Sproat-bend hooks. Hook sizes for trout run from size #10 to #2 and flies are tied in 2- to 4-inch lengths to imitate sizes of shiners, dace, chubs, smelt and shad. However, mega-designs use 1/0 to 5/0 size and the flies are 5 to 10 inches in total length.

Bucktail streamers imitate baitfish such as shiners and dace and are distinguished by their bodies, which are made of the hair from a whitetail buck.

tive materials become available. These space-age new streamers are often very effective big trout producers. Just keep in mind that the older standards like Bumblepuppies, Mickey Finns, Blacknose Dace, and Trudes are still great choices for success with those same big trout. I've always believed that those flies that best imitate the natural food trout depend on every day or season will be the most consistent producers of selective mature wild trout, char, and salmon.

This plate of classic bucktail streamers that I've chosen and illustrated for you includes the earliest, the most classic, and some of the most beautiful, and more current designs that are bound for classic reputations. My artistic skills were delightfully challenged by the unique form, color, pattern, and shape of hair. I've endeavored to give these bucktail portraits a semiwet appearance as a compromise between their unruly dry hair look and the streamline wet look. I hope they catch both your eye for their beauty as well as your fly-fishing imagination.

To further your bucktail streamer knowledge and tying skills I recommend:

> *Streamers & Bucktails—the Big Fish Flies* by Joseph D. Bates, Jr. (Alfred Knopf, 1980).
> *Streamer Tying and Fishing* by Joseph D. Bates, Jr. (Stackpole Books, 1966).

CHAPTER 33

CLASSIC NO-HACKLES

The classic no-hackles are a group of aquatic insect flies that imitate surface emergers and adult flies but do not use traditional stiff hackles to achieve surface flotation. No-hackles were conceived, designed, tested, and popularized in the 1960s and 1970s by Dr. Carl Richards and Doug Swisher. When their revolutionary book *Selective Trout* introduced no-hackles to the sport in 1971, their work created a sensation and revolution among dry-fly trout flyfishers across North America and Europe. Soon, even the most skeptical dry-fly purists began to see that no-hackles were almost irresistible to the most selective, surface-feeding trout. I remember thinking later that no-hackles were looked upon much like the Beatles were by the older generation when they first burst onto the scene . . . with much disdain.

Carl and Doug's designs soundly embraced the well-accepted surface imitation principle that trout mainly key in on the *silhouette* of the body and wings and on the color of the *underbody* and wings. These were believed—and correctly so—to be the most important colors of the overall pattern of an insect imitation. In fact, Carl and Doug named most of their patterns by

The concept of the Swisher-Richards no-hackle, surface-floating flies. Left to right: nymphal-shuck surface emerger, new emerger dun, natural mayfly shuck and adult, upright winged dun or spinner, spent winged spinner. Each of these flies rests on the surface film with help from their buoyant and waterproof dubbed bodies, wing positions, and tails. Extralight wire hooks further enhance their ability to float.

these two areas: slate-wing olive; gray-wing tan; cream-wing yellow. Legs and tails of naturals are not considered as critical to imitate in order to attract trout.

If there are not stiff hackle barbs to slow the descent of the fly to the water surface and then help it cling to the surface film, then how does a no-hackle float on the surface as do living mayflies and caddis? Carl and Doug simply designed their flies with extralight buoyant wing and body materials and used extra-fine-wire hooks. Carl wouldn't even use cement because it added extra weight. They also adjusted the center of gravity of their flies by positioning the wings and tails to hold the fly upright in the surface film. Most of the fly bodies were constructed of rough dubbing blends of buoyant polypropylene yarn, beaver belly, and water-resistant rabbit underfur. The tiny wild dubbing barbs in these blends are especially sticky to the water surface film, helping the flies to ride correctly in the water.

No-hackles are not designed to be used in fast, broken, freestone streams, but rather in waters like spring creeks, limestone creeks, river pools, and tailwaters, such as the Henry's Fork Harriman section, that have slow, glassy surfaces and hold the most selective, hatch-feeding trout. In these conditions, no-hackles will almost always outfish everything but live emergers, duns, and spinners!

My first experience using no-hackles was on a typical gray and chilly April opening day on Michigan's Au Sable River along a stretch where Carl had a cabin. There was a sparse emergence of Blue Wing Olives. I tried my best blue-dun and olive-hackled dry fly and only got two or three splashy refusals. Carl came to the rescue and gave me four of his size 18, duck-quill wing, BWO no-hackle Sidewinders to use. For several casts I could not see my fly. Then a nice trout softly rose at about the spot I thought my fly might be. Next thing I realized it had taken my no-hackle, hooked itself, and taken off. I got a rash of goose bumps! Two things became immediately apparent to me. Carl's no-hackles looked so much like the naturals, I couldn't see the difference

Starting at top, left to right (opposite page):

Row 1: Mayfly dun—no-hackles
    Duck Shoulder Tan.
    Duck Segment Olive.
    Mayfly Dun (natural).
    Duck Feather Segments Tan.
    Deer Hair Olive.
Row 2: Mayfly surface emergers—no-hackles
    Duck Segment Yellow-Olive.
    Mayfly Emerger with Nymphal Skin (natural).
    PMD Shuck.
    Z-Lon Shuck CDC Olive.
Row 3: Down-wing mayfly spent spinners—No-Hackles
    Hen Neck Rusty.
    Mayfly Spent Spinner (natural).
    Partridge Rusty.
Row 4: Additional spent mayflies—no-hackles
    Dun Hackle Yellow.
    Poly Golden Brown.

Row 5: At rest, tent-wing adult caddis—no-hackles
    Elk Hair Olive.
    Hen Back Tan-Olive.
    Adult Caddis (natural).
    Mottled Turkey Secondary Tan-Olive.
    Hen Hackle Tape Wing Olive.
Row 6: Spent-Winged Adult Caddis—no hackles (underwater view)
    Quad Partridge Tan-Olive.
    Spent Caddis (natural).
    Quad Hen Hackle Brown—Olive.
Row 7: Mayfly dun variations by other tiers
    Comparadun—Caucci-Nastasi design
Slate Olive Green Drake Paradun (larger, heavier mayfly dun with parachute hackle to improve flotation in more turbulent streams).
Cut Wing Hex Paradun (larger, heavier mayfly duns with parachute hackle to improve flotation in more turbulent streams.

nor could the Au Sable brown. The rise form to it was just like the rises to the naturals, not the splashy refusals to my original hackled flies I'd used earlier.

In almost all of my dry fly, match-the-hatch experiences with hackled dries, the trout takes looked different than those that trout made to the naturals, and I had accepted this as normal—along with years of high-percentage refusals. It was on that cloudy, cold, April opener when Carl gave me those "magic flies" that he also gave me a power I'd never known to catch highly selective wild trout feeding on mayflies, caddis, and midges!

Over the next years after that experience, I had the opportunity to test no-hackles across North America and in the British Isles, Yugoslavia, Germany, and South America. I had excellent success nearly everywhere I tried them and had a wonderful time sharing their magic with my guides and hosts. I also became close friends with Carl and Doug. I often referred to them as the "no-hackle twins" because, even though they were very different physically and in their temperament, they had identical beliefs about fly tying and fishing for selective trout.

About the same time that Carl and Doug were working on their no-hackle designs, several other inventive flyfishers were experimenting with the concept. *Hatches*, written by Al Caucci and Bob Nastasi, was published in 1975 and reprinted in 1986 and is the other major book on selective trout. Al and Bob's classic hackle-less Comparadun designs are still very effective and popular with trout anglers.

I might add that Carl and Doug, when testing no-hackles over several years on the Henry's Fork and Snake River near Last Chance, Idaho, became friends with local fly tiers and phenomenal selective-trout flyfishers Mike Lawson and René and Bonnie Harrop. Carl and Doug taught them how to tie the no-hackles, and these three went on to set today's standard of excellence with their professional ties of Doug and Carl's no-hackle and parachute designs—much like Elsie Darbee did for classic Catskill hackled dry flies. A Lawson or Harrop no-hackle in your hand or on the water will instantly give you the feeling of seeing a perfect representation of the no-hackle concept. Obtaining authentic samples of their artful versions or getting one of their tying DVDs is an absolute must if you want to tie no-hackles cor-

Left to right: No-hackle dry-fly flotation compared to cock-hackle, dry-fly flotation. The two flies on the left are classic dry flies that use cock hackle for flotation. In general, the hackle barbs above and below the surface do not assist in surface film support, only the barbs parallel to the water. The hackle can also obstruct the trout's view of the body and wings. The right two flies are no-hackle dry flies and adhere to the surface film with tails, wing bases, and dubbing fibers and allow an unobstructed view of the wings and body.

rectly. True, they are very simple flies, but tying them is not, and Mike or the Harrops can teach you to duplicate these most specific no-hackle designs.

When I learned they had plans to update *Selective Trout*, I offered to illustrate it in detailed, colored drawings. The second edition contains 178 of my illustrations and vividly supports the book's amazing, groundbreaking, and informative text and macrophotography. Carl and Doug were not the first or only fly tiers to experiment with the no-hackle concept of matching surface-floating mayfly emergers, duns, and spinners and caddis adults and midges, but they took the concept to a degree that gave us a complete working system, wrote the best-selling fly-fishing book in history, and made no-hackles a universally accepted standard system for selective trout.

To round out the selective dry fly examples, I've included illustrations of a few other currently popular, low-silhouette designs that float better on the higher-gradient, riffled surfaces of freestone streams. This is generally accomplished by trimming hackle barbs off the bottom of the fly, tying parachute hackles, or adding thorax hackles. On this fly plate I've included the water surface to give perspective to how the flies sit in the water.

Doug Swisher and Dr. Carl Richards forever changed how we can successfully approach the classic trout fly-fishing challenge of how to match floating aquatics that selective trout are rising to. One of my most cherished experiences in this sport was being friends and associates with the no-hackle twins and tying, illustrating, and fishing these classic no-hackles!

Suggested reading:
Selective Trout by Carl Richards and Doug Swisher, second edition, illustrated by Dave Whitlock (Skyhorse Publishing, 2017).

CHAPTER 34

THE INCREDIBLE MUDDLER MINNOW

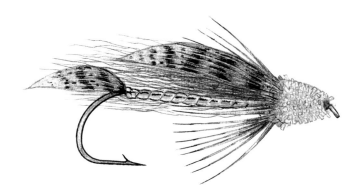

The Muddler Minnow is a flared deer hair, fat-headed streamer fly originally conceived by Don Gapen in 1936 while fishing below Virgin Falls on the Nipigon River, north Ontario's brook trout haven. Don's guide showed him how deadly live cockatush (sculpins) were on the seven- and eight-pound brookies. Don then produced a tying kit from his pack and, on the canoe's thwart, tied the first Muddler Minnow to imitate these sculpins. He not only created a killer fly for those Nipigon giants, but also an eighty-year fly revolution for catching big trout on the Muddler all around the world.

News of the Muddler Minnow's success spread rapidly, and many noted northeastern flyfishers and fly-fishing writers praised its effectiveness. Al (A. J.) McClane and Joe Brooks, two of the most highly skilled and respected writers, penned magazine and book features about this fly and were probably most responsible for its eventual worldwide appeal as a very effective pattern for big trout of all species, Atlantic salmon, steelhead, bass, and even saltwater species. It may be interesting to note that there are actually more types of sculpin in saltwater than fresh.

When Joe Brooks introduced the Muddler Minnow to Dan Bailey, Dan created his own version, as well as the Missoulian Spook and Marabou Muddler, and began making large numbers of this fly available to the public, along with many variations. This is when the popularity of the Muddler really took off, both nationally and internationally. Don's son, Dan, heads the Gapen Fly Company in Becker, Minnesota, and continues to produce his dad's design commercially. Don's original Muddler Minnow was tied on a 4X long, Allcock streamer hook using the body hair of whitetail deer for the head and collar, mottled turkey secondary feather for the wing, gray squirrel tail for the underwing, wide, flat, gold tinsel on the body, and the same mottled turkey quill for the tail.

Bailey's version, tied on a Mustad 9673, 3XL, substitutes white and brown calf tail for the underwing and made the deer-hair head denser and more neatly trimmed. Also, Bailey used more intricately marked and mottled turkey for the wing and tail. I'd describe Bailey's Muddler as being more neatly tailored than Don's. Although the original color pattern of dun gray, mottled

brown, and gold is still the most popular color and most correctly suggestive, Muddlers are tied in a variety of white, black, yellow, brandy brown, and olives. The live sculpin has an exquisitely detailed, camo-marked body that, just like a chameleon's, changes to whatever the colors are of the stream bottom where they live.

Although the Muddler Minnow was originally tied as a minnow streamer fly that suggests sculpins, gobies, darters, stonecats, suckers, and chubs, it is often used as a surface fly to imitate grasshoppers, cicadas, and adult stoneflies. Joe Brook's favorite hopper fly was a Bailey's Muddler Minnow dressed with floatant. Fishing it at the surface makes it a very effective waker for salmon and steelhead, with or without a riffle hitch. It's also a popular night fly, especially when tied with black deer hair and silver tinsel.

I've never heard anyone disagree that the Muddler's most important part is the spun and flared deer-hair head and collar. It looks so natural, seems to feel like food to fish, has a wide, low-frequency sound profile, and excellent water movement. Fish will actually try to eat a Muddler-headed fly as if it were live food. The magic of the flared deer-hair head is that you can improve almost any fly design by adding a Muddler head . . . from flies sized 5/0 down to size 16. Dan Baily's Missoulian Spook and Marabou Muddler as well as Donnie William's Spuddler are very effective Muddler-head spin offs. I truly believe that flared deer-hair has an almost mystical attraction to fish, and that's why I created both my Dave's Hopper and Matuka Sculpin using Muddler heads and collars. Troth's Bullhead had a very neat shape and trim and was also a big influence for me and helped lead me to develop a method of using multiple colors for the head—deer hair stacking and flaring—that gives us the ability to realistically match the sculpin's intricate head color pattern.

A buoyant Muddler can be made even more effective as a sculpin imitation by weighting the hook shank with wire, metal beads, cone heads, lead-headed jig hooks, or split shot and/or by fishing it on a short leader and sinking-tip or full-sink fly line. These will quickly sink the Muddler close to the bottom where trout most often encounter sculpins that live and scurry around on the stream bottom much more than they suspend above it. One of Joe Brooks's favorite ways to fish the Muddler Minnow was to add floatant to the head, cast it up and across-stream, and then fish it on a natural drift at the surface until it was well downstream. He would then pull it under and give it various swimming retrieves. Joe fully understood the awesome versatility of this fly! One of my favorite memories from when I was much younger is watching Joe fishing Muddler Minnows for big, hook-jawed, fall browns on the Big Hole and Yellowstone Rivers on ABC's *American Sportsman* television series.

Don Gapen's revolutionary Muddler Minnow gets my vote for our most effective trout fly

(Opposite page.) *Row 1:* Sculpin—Cottidae family. Common names are Muddler, miller's thumb, bullhead, cockatouch/cockatush. Side view, front, top.
Row 2: Dan Gapen's original Muddler Minnow. Side view, front, top.
Row 3: Dan Bailey's Muddler and variations: Missoulian Spook, Muddler Minnow, White Marabou Muddler.
Row 4: Three Muddler spinoffs, two Kennebago Muddlers (drake emergers by Brett Dam used mainly in Rangely Region of Maine), Atlantic Salmon Muddler Minnow, Conehead Muddler Minnow.
Row 5: Al Troth's Bullhead, Dave Whitlock's Matuka Sculpin, Spuddler: Donnie Williams/Dan Bailey.
Row 6: Danny Byford's Muddler Zonker.
Row 7: Muddler Periodic Cicadid, Dave's Hopper (Dave Whitlock), Muddler Adult Stonefly, Hornberg Muddler—Frank Horberg (Dave Whitlock added a Muddler head).
Row 8: Midnight Muddler (Dave Whitlock).

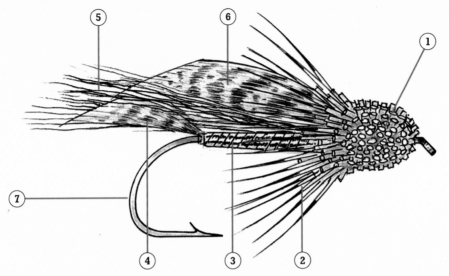

Diagram for the Parts of a Muddler Minnow Fly

1. **Muddler head:** One-third of the hook's shank. Material is body hair of whitetail or mule deer, spun around hook shank, then flared, trimmed and shaped.

2. **Muddler collar:** The untrimmed tips of the deer body hair that was used to form the muddler head. Lengths can be variable and average about one-half hook shank length.

3. **Body:** Flat, gold tinsel or dubbing ribbed with the same tinsel.

4. **Tail:** Paired sections of mottled turkey secondary wing quills. Tail length approximately one-third length of hook.

5. **Underwing:** Gray squirrel tail hair or gray fox tail hair. Length is equal to hook length.

6. **Wing:** Matched pair of mottled turkey secondary wing feather sections. Approximately three-fourths length of hook.

7. **Hook:** 3x or 4x long, turned-down-eye streamer hook in sizes 10 to 1/0.

design. The muddler and its family of variations and spinoffs are true classics. It's a design that, thanks to Don, Joe, and Dan, has enriched every trout flyfisher's world. It has also given fly tiers a design that can be infinitely varied to create more and more effective trout flies for as long as we fish for big trout, char, and salmon.

There's a current commercial that always concludes with "What's in your wallet?" I'd ask a similar question: "Are there Muddlers in your fly box?" An assortment of Muddlers will empower you to catch more large trout wherever you are.

For a more thorough and historic coverage of the Muddler Minnow, I recommend Mike Valla's *The Founding Flies*, chapter 22 (Stackpole Books, 2013).

CHAPTER 35

THE UPRIGHT HAIR-WING DRY FLY

The classic "upright hair-wing dry fly" is a heavily dressed, floating fly that suggests a mayfly dun or spinner. It was originated in 1930 by Lee Wulff, mainly to fish the north-eastern US and Canadian fast-flowing, freestone rivers, such as the Esopus, the Au Sable, and the Salmon. In the eighty-seven years since Lee's hair-wing dry fly innovation, the design has become universally popular and easily qualifies as one of our true classic trout flies.

Lee wanted a fly that would float well in high-gradient, freestone streams and hold up to the heavy use of multiple trout catches per day. He chose coarse guard hair from the tail of the whitetail deer to make the two thick and bushy upright wings and tail. Prior to Lee's Hair Wings, most dry flies were tied using feathers for wings. This material choice was so unique that it began an entire new series of dry flies that are both classics and still popular today.

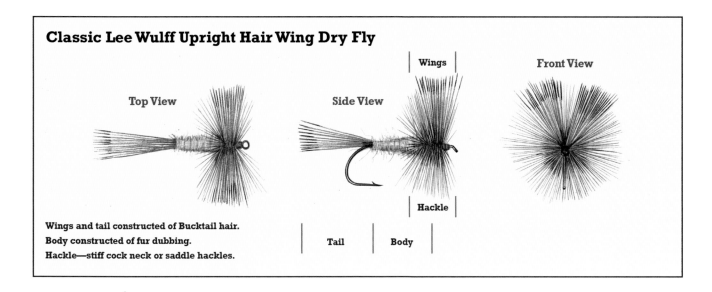

Classic Lee Wulff Upright Hair Wing Dry Fly

Top View

Side View

Wings

Front View

Hackle

Tail   Body

Wings and tail constructed of Bucktail hair.
Body constructed of fur dubbing.
Hackle—stiff cock neck or saddle hackles.

Two cock hackles and hair dubbing for a thick body completed his design. Lee's experiences with his first design—the Gray Wulff—came in the spring of 1930 while fly fishing with his friend Dan Bailey. The river was the Esopus and the results were dramatic—with Lee and Dan frequently landing over fifty trout a day on one fly!

Over the following decades, Lee and Dan continued to expand on Lee's incredibly productive hair-wing flies, and Dan insisted on calling them the "Wulffs." In 1938 Dan moved to Livingston, Montana, and began a fly-tying business. There he significantly expanded the Wulff pattern choices to take the best advantage of these special dry flies on the big, high-gradient western rivers that were heavily populated with lots of large, unselective (at that time) wild trout. These flies soon became some of the most productive dry flies for fast-flowing western rivers.

A list of these Wulff-Bailey-inspired flies includes: White Wulff, Royal Wulff, Black Wulff, Grizzly Wulff, Blonde Wulff, Ausable Wulff, and Brown Wulff. Although all these Wulff patterns were not necessarily tied to be imitations of specific mayfly duns and spinners, several are often used during mayfly hatches with good results, especially the Gray, White, and Grizzly Wulffs. Other tiers have since created more Wulff design patterns, good examples being the Humpy and Mike Lawson's Green Drake Wulff.

Lee was constantly innovating throughout his life. Trout, steelhead, landlocked and anadromous Atlantic salmon, bass, and sunfish are all very attracted to what Lee called his "meaty flies." Many Atlantic salmon flyfishers use Royal Wulffs and White Wulffs exclusively when dry fly fishing for Atlantic salmon. Lee's own ties of his Wulffs appear somewhat shaggy, with irregular wings, tails, and hackle barbs. This may be because Lee

tied them without a vise. I once watched Lee tie a size 20 Royal Wulff with just his fingers to hold the minuscule hook! The Wulffs that were tied at Dan Bailey's shop looked much more formal and symmetrical. I've illustrated both "looks" in the fly plate.

As I've stated earlier, stiff cock-hackle collar barbs that extend horizontally to the hook shank help a dry fly to sit or float in the surface film, while the barbs that extend up and down the hook shank do very little to help flotation. Because the Wulffs are usually tied with one or two long hackles, there are plenty of horizontal barbs to hold the fly at the surface, even in rough water. The thick, stiff hair of the tail also helps the fly float to a certain extent. Regularly treating these patterns with paste fly floatant and false casting a time or two to shake some of the water off also significantly improves flotation. Lee favored guard hairs from whitetail deer for most of his patterns. However, when white wings are required, calf tail is often used. Moose and elk hair can be used as good wing and tail substitutes, as well as the tail guard hairs of most game animals such as fox, mink, raccoon, squirrel, and otter.

It may be that the question "What in the world does this imitate?" is asked more about the extremely popular Royal Wulff than any other trout fly. The answer seems to be that it imitates nothing natural, but it can easily be *seen* by trout, as well as flyfishers, who can then mend and track it much better than dry flies that are a challenge to follow on the water. When tied in sizes 10 to 6, it is an ideal "searching fly" for trout. Sizes 8 to 4 are excellent for salmon, steelhead, smallmouth, and bass. I know quite a few experienced flyfishers who use Royal Wulffs almost anytime they dry fly fish, even during hatches, with good enough results to satisfy them.

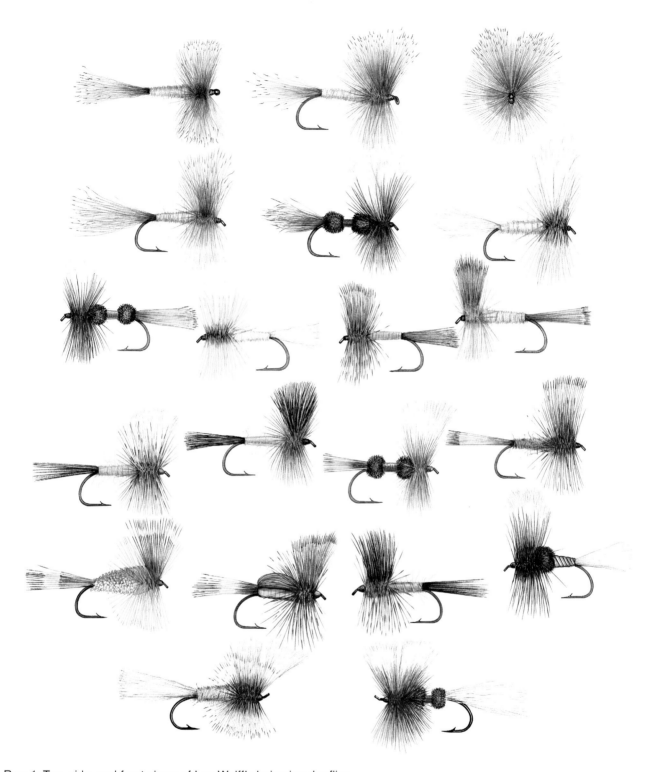

Row 1: Top, side, and front views of Lee Wulff's hair-wing dry flies.

Row 2: Original three Wulff hair-wing patterns tied by Lee without a vice: Gray Wulff, Royal Wulff, White Wulff.

Row 3: Dan Baily's commercially tied versions of Wulff hair-wings: Royal Wulff, White Wulff, Grizzly Wulff, Gray Wulff.

Row 4: Ausable Wulff, Black Wulff, Carolina Wulff, Blue Wulff, Adams Wulff.

Row 5: Four spinoff hair-wings: Messinger's Irresistible, Humpy, Lawson's Green Drake, H&R Variant.

Row 6: Lee Wulff's Atlantic salmon flies: White Wulff, Royal Wulff.

As with most successful fly designs, other tiers modify the Wulff designs, materials, and color schemes in order to have flies more specific for their situations. Some classic examples are the Humpy, Irresistible, H & R Variant, Lawson's Standard Green Drake, and Irresistible Wulff. I've added these variations or spinoffs to the color plate included here. As I was practicing my pen and pencil techniques to reproduce these classic patterns, I remembered an amusing experience. I wanted desperately to learn how to tie the Wulff patterns that looked like the nicely tied Dan Baily Wulff productions. I got the opportunity in 1961 to talk with Dan and Dan's shop manager Red Monical about the source of the uniquely marked bucktail wings and tails. They handed me a whitetail deer tail. I didn't believe them until Red showed me how they aligned all the bucktail tips. Suddenly the hair took on the completely different pattern and the neat look that I was after.

While recalling my experiences with Lee, I remembered a great example of Lee's awesome knowledge of catching Atlantic salmon on dry flies. At a fly fishing show in New York, while visiting with Lee, I told him that I was going to the Gaspé Peninsula to fish salmon on the St. Johns. He handed me a yellow, molded plastic and olive bucktail, parachute-hackled stonefly and told me it would work for me there. I was pleased. But I have to admit I wasn't very impressed with how it looked. Later, on the St. Johns, I cast for two hours over a very large, fresh-run female. She rose to several of my dry flies but simply nosed or

tailed them. In desperation, I tied on Lee's stonefly. On my first cast over this beautiful salmon, she rose vertically up from seven feet down and engulfed that fly as if she had waited all day for the opportunity! I didn't recover from the shock quite fast enough to deal with this magnificent twenty-pounder, and it soon broke me off at the end of a 10-foot leap. Lee knew dry fly salmon fishing!

Lee Wulff was one of my most cherished mentors, role models, and friends. His image and contributions in our sport will live forever. I urge you to read the reference materials that I've listed below to get a truly amazing picture of this very special, one-of-a-kind man. Besides his classic flies, he taught something that was almost unheard of at the time. His belief was that a wild, adult trout or salmon is a treasure that is too valuable to catch and kill because it represents the distillation of hundreds or thousands of its kin's top gene pool for all future survival success. Not only was he 100 percent right in this belief, but he set the stage for one of the most important ethics of fly fishing: catch and release.

I highly recommend that you read about Lee's life story in these books:

The Founding Flies by Mike Valla (Stackpole, 2013).

Lee Wulff on Flies by Lee Wulff (Stackpole Books, 1985).

The Complete Lee Wulff by Lee Wulff (Dutton, 1989).

CHAPTER 36

SMALL CRUSTACEAN FLIES

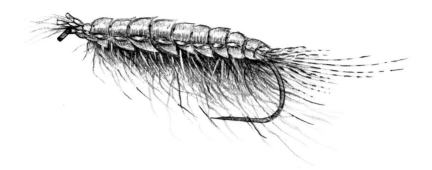

There are five small freshwater crustacean groups in North America that are of interest to flyfishers. These tiny invertebrates inhabit calcium carbonate–rich streams, rivers, tailwaters, and lakes and are an especially nutrient-rich food form for trout. Imitating these five groups—scuds (Amphipoda), shrimp (Decapoda), opossum shrimp (Mysidacea), water fleas or Daphnia (Cladocera), and sow bugs (Isopoda)—is simple and easy because crustaceans have only one form to imitate in various colors and sizes. Having many generations each year, they are often found in large numbers, and this abundance offers trout a year-round source of nutritious food. Trout with access to crustaceans usually grow quickly, have lots of energy, and develop richly colored bodies with dark salmon-colored flesh.

So, folks, here's a brief introductory profile of each of these crustacean groups:

1. Scuds (Amphipoda). Other names: shrimp, freshwater shrimp, sideswimmers, and gammarus.

Scuds are usually one-quarter to three-quarter inches (6.4 to 19 mm) with occasional maximum size over one inch. There are four body color phases—gray, tan, olive, and yellow—

that are intricately marked. The coloring varies, depending on diet and environment. If the stomach contents of a trout are sampled, most of the scuds will be orange because as they die, they turn various shades of orange. The natural colors are what selective feeders are most interested in, but orange and red scud flies can be useful as attractor flies or salmon egg flies.

Scuds are active crawlers and bottom swimmers and look a bit rambunctious as they tumble and swim in their nearly constant foraging and mating activities. Scuds have multiple broods each year that are produced mostly between April and November. To fish scud flies, just allow them to sink to or near the bottom and let them drift and tumble downstream or, in still waters, retrieve them slowly with short, irregular line strips and very subtle rod-tip twitches. If you use strike indicators, make sure there is enough tippet length between the indicator and the scud to allow the fly to sink close to the bottom.

2. Shrimp (Decapoda). Other names: freshwater shrimp and freshwater prawns.

Adults are one-quarter inch to one inch (6.4 to 25 mm) long and are usually varying tints of gray or olive. They look and actively swim much like

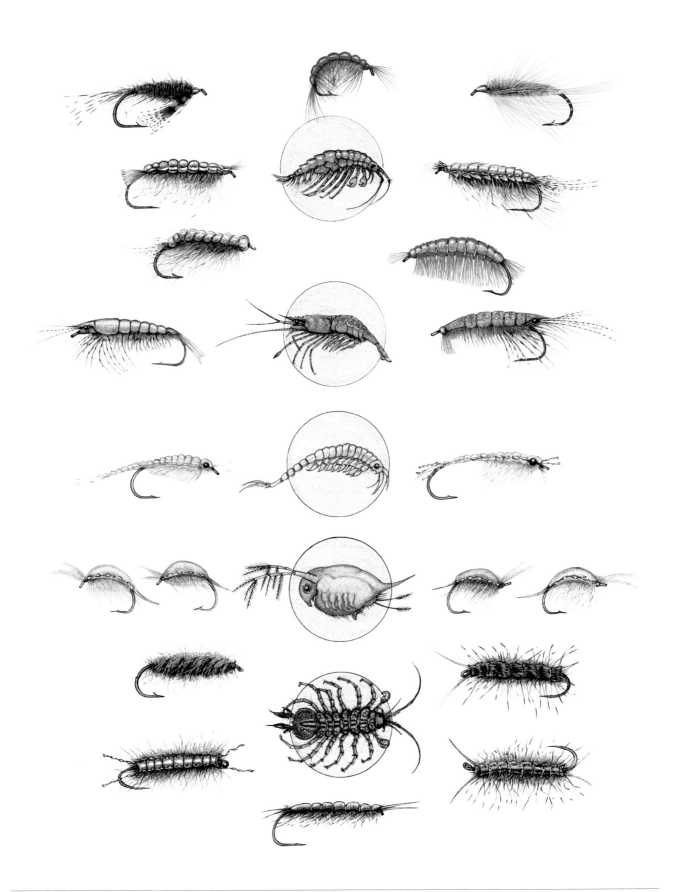

their cousins—saltwater shrimp—but live mainly in ponds, sloughs, canals, and lakes and are often misidentified as scuds. Shrimp are easy to imitate and fish, and you'll get the best results if you twitch these flies erratically through the water column similar to scuds.

3. Opossum Shrimp (Mysidacea). Other names: backswimmers, ghost shrimp, and Mysis.

Most Mysis shrimp inhabit the lower levels of deep, cold lakes and are often flushed into the tailwaters below such lakes that have dams. At one-third inch to one inch, these tiny, ghostly white or cream-colored shrimp are important to lake trout but also contribute to tailwater browns, rainbows, cutthroat, and cutbows growing to trophy size. A prime example is the tiny Frying Pan creek tailwater between the dam and the confluence with the Roaring Fork River near Aspen and Basalt, Colorado. It annually produces Mysis-fed trophies that top the size list in the state. The best times to fish tailwater Mysis are in winter, spring, and late fall when the water is being released or for short periods afterward. Fish Mysis imitations at the speed and direction of the current and close to the bottom, using very light tippet and small, sensitive indicators.

4. Water Fleas or Daphnia (Cladocera).

Water fleas are the smallest of these five crustaceans, with their length up to one-eighth inch (0.2 to 3.2 mm). But in many small, high-altitude lakes, they are often the most prolific trout food, occurring in great abundance. In such lakes, trout feed most often near the surface in late afternoon and evening, as the water fleas swim upward at this time of day, and at early light before the fleas swim back down to lower light levels. Flyfishers who are not aware of the presence of these tiny organisms, fish the wrong time of day, or do not have adequate imitations can come away frustrated. Their colors range widely, from almost transparent to tans, olives, reds, blues, and greens. Imitating them requires tying a simple, compact, fur dubbing form on hook sizes 18 to28.

Small crustacean flies (opposite page):

Row 1: Group—Scuds
1. Trueblood's Otter Shrimp.
2. Orange Curved Scud.
3. Polly Rosborough Shrimp.

Row 2: Group—Scuds
1. Randall Kaufman's Flashback Scud.
2. Natural Scud (Amphidoda).
3. Whitlock's Swimming Scud.

Row 3: Group—Scuds
1. Beadhead Scud.
2. Big Horn or Canyon Ferry Orange Shrimp.

Row 4: Group—Freshwater Shrimp
1. Freshwater Shrimp.
2. Natural Freshwater Prawn (Decapoda).
3. Whitlock's Backward Swimming Freshwater Shrimp.

Row 5: Group—Opossum Shrimp
1. Shane Stalcup's Mysis Shrimp.
2. Natural Opossum or Mysis Shrimp (Mysidacea).
3. Roy Palm's Shellback Mysis Shrimp.

Row 6: Group—Daphnia or Water Fleas
1. Tan Daphnia Fly.
2. Red Daphnia Fly.
4. Natural Daphnia or Water Flea (Cladocera).
5. Blue-Green Daphnia.
6. Gray Daphnia.

Row 7: Group—Sow Bugs
1. Ed Shenk's Cress Bug.
2. Turkey Quill-Back Sow Bug.

Row 8: Group—Sow Bugs
1. Natural Sow Bug (Isopoda).

Row 9: Group—Sow Bugs
1. Davy Wotton's Krystal Flash Sow Bug.
2. Whitlock's Up-Hook Crawling Sow Bug.

Row 10: Group—Sow Bugs
1. Side profile view of sow bug fly.

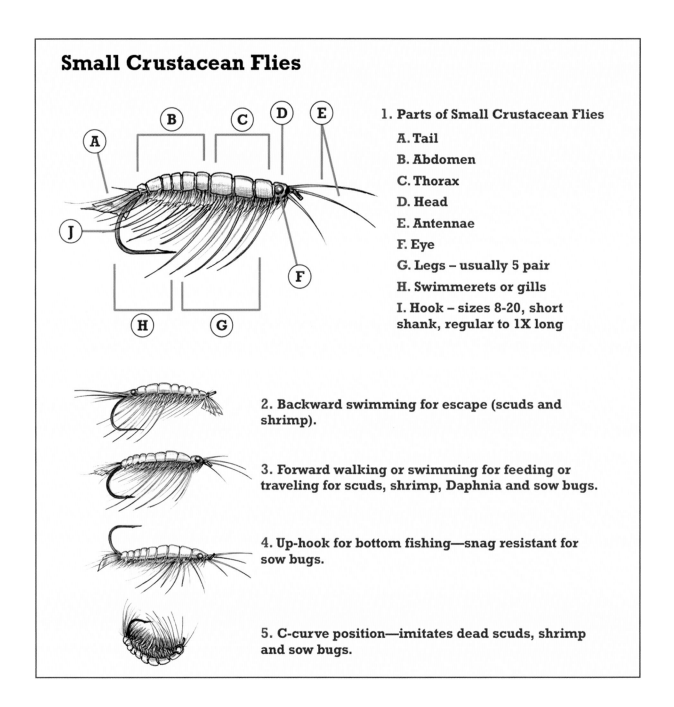

Small Crustacean Flies

1. Parts of Small Crustacean Flies

   A. Tail

   B. Abdomen

   C. Thorax

   D. Head

   E. Antennae

   F. Eye

   G. Legs – usually 5 pair

   H. Swimmerets or gills

   I. Hook – sizes 8-20, short shank, regular to 1X long

2. Backward swimming for escape (scuds and shrimp).

3. Forward walking or swimming for feeding or traveling for scuds, shrimp, Daphnia and sow bugs.

4. Up-hook for bottom fishing—snag resistant for sow bugs.

5. C-curve position—imitates dead scuds, shrimp and sow bugs.

5. Aquatic Sow Bugs (Isopoda). Other names: pill bugs, roly-polies, and cress bugs.

Sowbugs are one-quarter to three-quarter inches (6.4 to 19 mm) long and do not swim but slowly crawl along the bottom of their habitat, sometimes losing hold and tumbling downstream like tiny leaves. Sowbugs have a flat, distinctively segmented body, with numerous pairs of obvious appendages. This flat body design allows them to live even on the bottoms of fast-flowing streams. Most are mottled grays with hints of tan or olive on their backs and light gray or whitish on the underside.

Imitating sowbugs is quite simple, as is fishing them close to the bottom, dead-drifting with the current speed and direction. Casting to sighted fish or drifting with small strike indicators are the two most consistent ways to fish them. Sowbugs are not as well distributed as scuds, although they often coinhabit with scuds in streams that are very rich in calcium carbonate and aquatic plants. Such dual populations seem to produce almost constant trout-feeding activity. One of the most extreme examples of this is the Little Red River below Gerry's Ferry Lake in Arkansas. This sow bug and scud tailwater regularly produces wild browns that exceed twenty pounds. For some years it held the world-record brown—something just over forty pounds caught by Rip Collins. Rip told me a stomach contents analysis showed it contained just over two pounds of these crustaceans!

Small Crustacean Flies

In North America, tying and fishing small crustaceans was relatively late in development. It seems the mindset of fly fishing for trout was historically focused on aquatic insects. Plus, the waters rich in small crustaceans—mostly those with low-gradient flows of calcium carbonate–rich waters, such as springs, spring creeks, ponds, and small lakes, and at latitudes where waters are cold enough to be year-round trout habitat—are limited. Except for tailwaters, these mostly occur in spring-fed waters in a few Eastern states, the western Rocky Mountains, upper Midwest, and western Oregon and California.

The crustaceans I've listed are imitated by only one form—after hatching they don't change form, just size—and because they rarely exceed one inch, only two or three hook sizes scope their entire size range.

The first crustacean flies were credited to Ed Kock (pill bug) and Ed Shenk (cress bug) from the limestone creek area of Pennsylvania in the mid-1990s, Ted Trueblood (Ted's Otter Shrimp) from Idaho, and Polly Rosborough (Polly's Shrimp) from Oregon. The crustaceans these tiers imitated were predominantly sow bugs and scuds.

The basic small crustacean imitation requires that they be constructed on small, short-shank, regular and 1X shank hooks and materials that are water absorbent, translucent, and have soft textured dubbing (such as underbody fur of otter, muskrat, rabbit, or mink), soft bird feathers, and, for the back of the fly, latex, polypropylene, or feather sections. Segmentation is usually accomplished with plastic-coated wire or tying thread. Lead or copper wire and/or metal beads are used to give the flies the weighting necessary to sink them quickly to or near the bottom. An excellent, all-purpose body material is a blend of otter, muskrat, or beaver-belly underfur, red or gray squirrel back hair, and Antron dubbing. The brindle or variegated color pattern and length of squirrel back makes it ideal for suggesting legs, swimmerets, and antennae when blended with these underfurs and Antron. To have a full range of colors this blend should be made up in gray, pale olive, tan, and orange.

Small crustacean flies are most effective imitations when fished just above the bottom with slow movements or with bottom-current speeds. My favorite way to fish scuds and sow bug flies is to weight them in a manner so they sink, but not anchor, and just swim or crawl over the bottom structure. Most of these weighted flies I've illustrated fish with the hook up so they don't easily catch on the bottom. I use a distance between a very small-sized, mute-colored indicator and the fly that allows the fly to always be next to the bottom as the water depths vary. This tippet length is usually about 4 to 6 feet in most riffles, runs, and heads of pools. Fluorocarbon in sizes

5, 6, and 7X is my favorite tippet for fishing these flies.

These crustacean flies are always effective, year-round producers wherever there are populations of them. The waters that contain crustaceans produce daily feeding activity, especially by larger, well-conditioned trout, char, and grayling, and you may find that a crustacean imitation can easily become your go-to fly.

For more detailed small crustacean information, I recommend:

Nymphs by Ernest Schwiebert (New Win Publishing).

Aquatic Entomology by W. Patrick McCafferty (Jones & Bartlett Learning, 1983).

Freshwater Invertebrates by Robert W Pennak (John Wiley & Sons Inc., 1978).

Whitlock's Guide to Aquatic Trout Foods by (Dave Whitlock Lyons Press, 1992).

The classic feeding position for trout on bottom-dwelling crustaceans such as sowbugs.

THE FLAT HAIR-WINGS

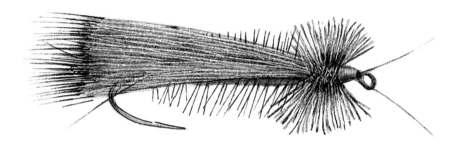

The flat hair-wing is a classic dry-fly design that is mainly used to imitate adult stoneflies at rest but also mimics adult dobsonflies and caddis, grasshoppers, cicadas, and wasps. It can be a useful searching fly any time of the year. This design was one of the later North American contributions to dry-fly fishing because stoneflies were generally ignored in the earlier days of fly fishing in the Eastern states, as there was such an abundance of mayfly hatches

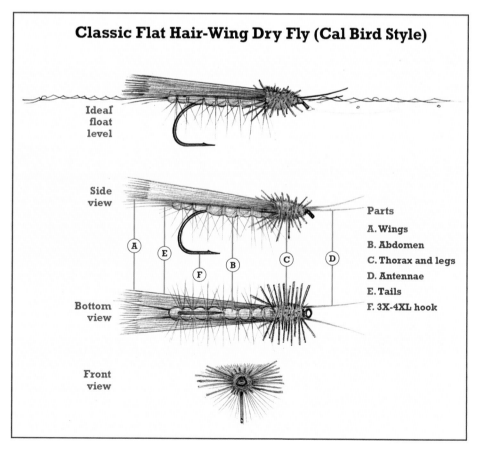

Classic Flat Hair-Wing Dry Fly (Cal Bird Style)

Ideal float level

Side view

Bottom view

Front view

Parts
A. Wings
B. Abdomen
C. Thorax and legs
D. Antennae
E. Tails
F. 3X-4XL hook

One of the more recent North American contributions to dry-fly fishing, the flat hair-wings imitate stoneflies at rest, plus adult dobsonflies and caddis, grasshoppers, cicadas, and even wasps.

and so many popular mayfly imitations brought over from England. Eastern and Midwestern trout streams also seemed to have fairly small stonefly populations, with many hatching after dark. Several of these stonefly species have nymph forms that crawl out of the water to emerge rather than emerging through the water surface. On the other hand, stoneflies often hatch in huge numbers in the Rocky Mountain states and West Coast rivers, where they are usually daylight emergers.

It is a reasonable guess that flat hair-wing stonefly designs first made an appearance in North America between 1900 and 1930. At least we know that Ray Bergman, Lee Wulff, Chauncy Lively, Cal Bird, and George Grant were all alive within that period and all created versions of adult stoneflies using the flat hair-wing profile. I've illustrated each of these on the first rows of the fly plate. It is frequently true that a need or opportunity is often addressed by others before or simultaneously with those who are better known, so there may well have been tiers that developed this type of fly in North America that we don't know about.

Of these early patterns, my favorite has always been the Bird's Stonefly, as Cal Bird truly captured the essence and anatomy of a surface-riding adult stonefly. It is functionally realistic and an excellent trout catcher and is easily the symbol of this classic stonefly design from this artist and flyfisher's perspective.

Mike Lawson's flat-wings are perhaps the best of the new versions of adult stoneflies. Mike has a special talent for creating flies that are effective and good-looking, and he has lots of stream experience fishing on arguably the best stonefly river on this continent—the Box Canyon of the Snake River.

The flat hair-wing dry fly was originally constructed with whitetail deer bucktail guard hairs. In recent years, elk hair has become most widely used to construct the wings because it is a long, coarse, and durable hair with enhanced flotation properties. The minor drawback to elk is that thread tends to compress the hair, and, if care is not taken, the hair will flare too much, causing the wings to look as though they were fluttering—more like a caddis profile or stonefly egg layer. It might be asked if feather or plastic wings are more realistic. Perhaps, but they lack the durability and flotation of coarse hairs.

Squirrel tail, woodchuck, fox, and coyote tail guard hairs, as well as moose, are also acceptable hairs. However, since these hairs are only mildly buoyant, cock hackle, deer, or elk hair are often

Flat hair wings (opposite page, left to right):

Row 1
1. Tiny early black stonefly (Taeniopterygidae).
2. Early brown stonefly (Taeniopterygidae).
3. Giant salmon fly (Pteronacys Californica).
4. Olive stonefly (green or yellow) (Chloroperlidae).
5. Big golden stonefly (Perlidae).
6. Tiny yellow Sally (Isoperla Patricia).

Row 2
1. Ray Bergman's Stonefly.
2. Lee Wulff's plastic body, parachute stonefly.
3. Michigan Stone—Chauncy Lively and Paul Young.
4. Chuck Caddis—Eric Leiser.

Row 3
1. Golden adult stone—Polly Rosborough.
2. Bird's Dark Stonefly—Cal Bird.
3. Trude Stonefly—George Grant.

Row 4
1. Dark Stonefly or Salmon fly—Andre Puyans.
2. Whitlock Dark Stone adult—Dave Whitlock.
3. Lawson's Box Canyon Dark Stone—Mike Lawson.

Row 5—More recent designs
1. Schlotter's Rogue Foam Parastone (Big Golden)—Jack Schlotter.
2. Kaufman's Orange Seducer—Randall Kaufmann.
3. Rainy's Foam Gorilla Stonefly—Jesse Rainy.

used at the head and thorax areas to improve the flotation that is required in the rough surface and swifter current typical of the waters that stoneflies inhabit. In torrent rivers like the Madison and Yellowstone, I've sometimes seen the Sofa Pillow tied with three or four cock hackles for flotation. In my opinion, flared and trimmed muddler-type heads and collars or bullet heads and collars are superior to cock hackles.

The bodies of the early designs were often made of elk rump hair, yarns, floss, and palmered cock hackles. More recently, plastic foam strips have become popular. Even though foam is a bit more practical and easier to tie, I still love to make segmented, extended stonefly adult bodies out of elk rump hair—it's just such a classic look to me. I also feel that the heavier weight of flies tied with hair makes them land on the surface with the natural *plop* sound of a living stonefly. Lee Wulff tied his bucktail, flat-wing stonefly using a molded plastic body and a parachute hackle. Over the last decade, some flat-wing designs are being tied with the parachute hackle that Lee introduced to improve flotation over the more traditional hook-shank hackling. The tails and antennae of flat wings can be realistically duplicated with hackle stems or biots of goose or turkey primary wing quills. Moose and elk mane hairs are also ideal.

The long, robust bodies of stoneflies are usually constructed on long shank—3X or 4X lengths are most common. My favorites are the TMC 5263 and TMC 300. The most common sizes are 8, 6, 4, and 2. Body colors range among dark brown, orange, yellow, light olive, brown, tan, cream, dun gray, and light gray cream. The stonefly adults at the top of my fly plate depict the natural color range. Because flat hair-wing dries can be a bit difficult to see and track on typical stonefly-rich rivers, many modern versions now often have white or fluorescent tufts of yarn, hair, or foam protruding up above the thorax to significantly enhance their visibility for flyfishers.

One of our most recent classic fly designs, the flat hair-wing dry fly is a fascinating trout fly that seems to be constantly evolving, especially those tied to be used on the Rocky Mountain and West Coast tumbling, rock and boulder freestone rivers. Trout, char, steelhead, and Atlantic salmon all rise to them so eagerly, and they are superb river smallmouth bass surface flies, as well—day and night.

I very much enjoy illustrating and tying flat-wings because I have years of very special memories of watching big trout inhale them off the surface.

I feel so fortunate to have had a life that allowed me the experiences and the time to develop the knowledge and skills to compose and illustrate this book in a way that I hope has shown you the beauty I see in trout and their kin and in those wonderful feather and hair sculptures that allow us to so directly connect with these cold-water treasures. Em and I hope our book will help you embrace even more the value and blessings that we all share in this incredible sport of fly fishing.

—Dave